REMEMBERING DAVEY

PORTRAIT
OF AN AMERICAN HERO

Clyde Bolton
Mike Bolton

ISBN 0-9635413-1-5

Book Design and Layout: Lori Leath Smith

Printed by Ebsco Media
Birmingham, Alabama

Copies of this book may obtained from:
The Birmingham News
Division of Special Projects
P.O. Box 2553
Birmingham, AL 35202
(205) 325-3188

Table of Contents

Dedication

To Krista Marie and Robbie Grey

With our sincerest hope that this book will help preserve the memories of your father—his determination, fairness, competitive spirit, love of life and concern for others.

And to all who are part of the Alabama Gang family,
May you have peace.

Foreword

Davey Allison was a very special person who touched the lives of many people. That was never more evident than on July 15 when hundreds of people lined the roads to hold signs and wave good-bye on the route from the church to the cemetery.

He touched a lot of lives in a positive way. We will all miss him.

Davey's life can never be replaced, but we are left with many good memories—many of which can be found in this book.

The Allison family would like to thank everyone—family, friends and fans—for their support of Davey through the years and the support they showed our family through hard times.

—Tommy Allison
general manager, Davey Allison Racing

Davey Allison had a short life, but it was a full life—and not just for himself, for he cared for and did a lot for other people.

His death brought a great outpouring of love for Davey and the Allison family. It was touching to see how much he meant to so many people. You get notes from people saying, "We're pulling for you," and maybe you're busy and don't think a lot about it—but this makes you think about it.

Some might think Davey had things handed to him because he was Bobby's son, but that's not true. Bobby made him work, often at the worst job at his shop.

Davey didn't win right off the bat. He struggled like everybody else. It's easy to build that race car one time, and it would be nice to have the luxury of it never tearing up. But race cars do tear up, and Davey worked hard to rebuild that car time after time.

I watched Davey go from being a kid playing racing to a serious racer to being a serious winner. I have no doubt he would have eventually won the Winston Cup championship, because you can't run at that level at which he was running without winning it.

It was bad enough losing a good friend, but we lost a good racer and a good ambassador to the sport.

I am glad that Davey's story is being told in words and pictures in this book by Clyde and Mike Bolton, who covered Davey's career from the very beginning through his years of Winston Cup stardom.

—Neil Bonnett

"They became short-track terrors, and one day when they pulled their three cars into the pits of a track in North Carolina, one of the local drivers groused, 'Oh, no, there's that Alabama Gang again.' The name stuck."

PROLOGUE

The Alabama Gang, yes. Davey Allison wasn't one of the original Gangsters—but he was proud to be included when he reached maturity.

This book pays tribute to a stock car racing star who died at the age of 32. On Monday, July 12, 1993, the helicopter that Davey Allison was flying crashed in the infield at Talladega Superspeedway. He died the next morning. Red Farmer, racer and Hueytown, Ala., neighbor, was injured but was dismissed from the hospital on Wednesday.

How did Davey Allison, who was born in Hollywood, Fla., on Feb. 25, 1961, come to live in Alabama? How did he come to live in Hueytown, the biggest little racing town in the U.S.A.? That in itself is a story.

Davey's father Bobby Allison, Bobby's brother Donnie Allison and Farmer were the original "gypsies" who came from Hialeah, Fla., to Hueytown. Short track racing wasn't much in South Florida, but it was strong in the Birmingham area. So they followed the smell of carbon monoxide and money.

And Alabama drivers did call them gypsies—sometimes with grudging admiration, sometimes just grudgingly.

Farmer smiled at the recollection. "They said we traveled like gypsies, and actually we did. The three of us would head off to Tennessee or somewhere in a caravan. I guess we looked like gypsies."

Bobby Allison told how the Hialeah-to-Hueytown odyssey began in 1959:

"The girlfriend of Gil Hearn, a friend of ours, moved to Jasper, Tenn. To have an excuse to go see his girlfriend, he talked another friend, Kenny Andrews, into loading up Andrews' race car and coming up to this area to find race tracks.

"They parked it in the girlfriend's yard and went and saw racing in Chattanooga and Huntsville, and they had heard about short tracks in Birmingham and Atlanta and Rome, Ga., and Montgomery. They never unloaded the car off the trailer, but they came home telling about all the tracks up here.

"We raced on Wednesday night in West Palm Beach. Red Farmer won, and I ran second. I had a handful of money and I said, "Hey, I'm going to Alabama.' Donnie said, 'I'm going with you.' Kenny and Gil said, 'We're going, too.'

"Donnie jumped in the truck with me, and Kenny and Gil got in their truck, and we left.

"We got to Dothan and stopped at a gas station and asked, 'Where are the race tracks?' The guy said, 'There aren't any here, but there's a nice one in Montgomery.'

"So we went to Montgomery. We saw a race car at a gas station and stopped and met Bo Freeman. He told us all about racing in the area.

"We met the promoter, and he said, 'We run tomorrow night, but they run tonight at Dixie Speedway in Midfield.' He called the promoter at Dixie, Big Hearted Eddie Wright, and he said come ahead.

"I ran fifth in the heat, fifth in the semi and fifth in the feature. I went to the pay window and thought I had died and gone to heaven. I told Donnie, 'We can get one of those $2 steaks and might even get a motel room to sleep in.'

"We went to Montgomery and ran second in the heat and second in the feature the next evening. I made over $300, and I was flabbergasted."

They were rained out at the Peach Bowl in Atlanta the next night, and they treked on to Jasper, Tenn., to see Gil Hearn's girlfriend. Bobby went to a speed shop "and spent some money on sure 'nuff racing parts instead of homemade ones."

He blew an engine at Dixie the next Friday night, borrowed some parts from Harry Mewbourne and repaired the engine in Bo Freeman's driveway. He scored his first Montgomery feature victory the next night.

"That same night," Bobby recalled, "Gil Hearn decided to quit Kenny Andrews, and Kenny put Donnie in the car. That really started Donnie's career. He had run some jalopies in Miami before that."

Bobby left the Peach Bowl the next evening and headed home "with $700 or $800 in my pocket. I ran into my buddy Red Farmer and told him he needed to load his stuff up and head for Alabama.

"Red was a journeyman electrician, working full-time. I convinced him he at least needed to take a vacation and go to Alabama.

"He came up and won eight straight features, and that's why most people remember him as being up here before I was. But that wasn't the case."

The Allison brothers and Farmer began commuting between home and the bullrings in Alabama, Georgia and Tennessee.

"It was a 24-hour trip from Miami," Farmer recalled. "There was no interstate. I'd go to Alabama and make some money and go back to Miami and live on it and go back to Alabama and make some more."

For one period, the Allison brothers and Farmer and their teams lived together in Birmingham.

"We got an apartment in a big old building in West End," Farmer recalled. "We had two bedrooms and a living room. Some slept on the floor and some on the couch. We took turns.

"There'd be three race cars parked out front and eight or nine of us in one apartment."

The Allisons and Farmer frequently finished 1-2-3. What had been a fun, semi-pro sport in the Birmingham area suddenly got more serious.

"We raced to survive," Farmer said of himself and the Allisons. "We didn't have other jobs. I think we were more dedicated than somebody racing for a hobby, as most of the local boys were. If we didn't go to the pay window, we couldn't feed our kids.

"Local drivers used to throw tires away, and we'd get them and sew them up with wire and put boots in them. Anytime they'd cut a tire, they'd give it to us."

Farmer was especially attracted to the Birmingham area.

"I was living on unemployment checks," he said. "They had trouble with the blockade of Cuba. I was an electrician, and building went to a standstill. We didn't know whether there was going to be a war. I had six dependents - me, my wife Joan, three kids and Joan's grandmother - and was making $33 a week unemployment. The only other thing I had was a race car."

The Allison brothers and Farmer tired of the commuting and in the early 1960s moved into the Birmingham area, soon landing in Hueytown.

Their racing identity became that of Alabamians, not Floridians. They became short-track terrors, and one day when they pulled their three cars into the pits of a track in North Carolina, one of the local drivers groused, "Oh, no, there's that Alabama Gang again." The name stuck.

Neil Bonnett became a Gangster in later years. Bobby Allison raced against him and was impressed with the youngster, eventually taking him on as a protege.

Bonnett and his wife Susan lived in Fairfield, another Birmingham suburb, "but after I got to fooling with race cars we moved to Hueytown," he explained.

"People don't understand about race cars," Bonnett said. "It isn't a 9-to-5 job. You work on race cars at night, sometimes all night. By living in Hueytown, I could just run over to Red's or Bobby's and borrow stuff."

Hueytown is not a logical place for a Winston Cup driver to call home. Charlotte is the hub of the sport, and many drivers move to that area.

But Davey Allison grew up in Hueytown, and there he stayed, building a fine house for himself and his family.

"It's not practical to live here," Bonnett admitted. "We've got to fly 500 miles just to get where the others start from.

"At one time, Charlotte was offering deals for teams, helping to locate land. I had an offer of land and a house. But this is home to me.

"I like to fish and hunt, and we're fortunate to have it all right here. Sometimes people in this area don't realize how fortunate they are."

Bobby Allison said he considered moving to the Charlotte area years ago, but his racing career was uncertain, what with losing rides, etc., "and I kept having to depend on the base I had in Hueytown.

"I had friends. Bo Fields was there. Tom Gloor was close by, and I leaned on him for advice. I had some businesses close by that supported me, like Tom Gloor Chevrolet and Long-Lewis Ford and Mulkin Auto Parts and Gibson Sheet Metal. When I needed something they would work an hour or two extra to see that I was on schedule. I didn't feel that closeness anywhere else."

Even after he began fielding his own team from a shop in the Charlotte area, Bobby Allison continued to live in Hueytown.

Davey Allison was born, fittingly, on the eve of the 1961 Daytona 500.

Bobby's brother-in-law, Ralph Stark, had built a Winston Cup car, and he asked Bobby if he'd like to drive it at Daytona. On Friday, Feb. 24, 1961, two days before the 500, Bobby made his first Winston Cup start, finishing 20th in a qualifying race and earning $50 and 36th starting position in Sunday's Daytona 500.

The qualifying event had barely ended when Bobby received a call that Judy was having the baby. He jumped into his red and white pickup truck and sped toward the Miami area. On Saturday he became the father of a boy they named David Carl.

Bobby stayed with Judy as long as he could, then drove back to Daytona, arriving in time to start the 500. He finished 31st, 25 laps behind, but running at the end.

But Davey wouldn't grow up a Floridian. In 1963 he and his parents moved to Hueytown, which would become the biggest little racing town in the land. Hueytown's reputation as the home of fiercely competitive race drivers already was made when Davey started competing. But he did his part to carry the flag, winning 19 Winston Cup races. He was as much a member of the Alabama Gang as any of the others.

"When Davey was less than one year old, he'd stand in the front seat of the pickup truck beside me at night on the way back from a race. Every once in awhile he'd kind of go 'udden…udden…'
I'd say 'That's it…attaboy…you got it.'"

—*Davey's father*

Chapter One

Boyhood Years

If Davey Allison wasn't born with racing in his blood, it didn't take long for it to get there. He arrived in this world on the eve of Bobby Allison's first Daytona 500. The dusty infields of race tracks across America soon became his playpen.

The nature of the auto racing family is much like that of the farming family. Tough times dictate a special family closeness, a dedication to get the job done no matter the obstacles or the hour. And just as the sons of farmers tend to follow in their fathers' footsteps, so do the sons of auto racing drivers.

Richard and Kyle Petty couldn't avoid the temptation of racing's call, nor could Dale Jarrett, Dale Earnhardt, Buddy Baker, Michael Andretti, Al Unser, Jr., Sterling Marlin or Larry Pearson.

And neither could Davey Allison.

"When Davey was less than one year old, he'd stand in the front seat of the pickup truck beside me at night on the way back from a race," Bobby remembers. "Every once in awhile he'd kind of go 'udden..udden...'

"I'd say 'That's it . . . attaboy . . . you got it.'"

Red Farmer, who was injured in Davey's fatal helicopter crash on July 12, 1993, has lived a few doors down from the Allisons on Church Street in Hueytown for almost 30 years. He remembers racing being in Davey's soul from the start.

"Davey was always a competitor," he said. "He and Clifford (Davey's brother) used to come into the shop on tricycles racing each other. We'd be there working on race cars, and we'd have to run them out.

"A few years later, they'd come racing through there on bicycles."

Tommy Allison, Jr., Davey's cousin, lived in Miami in Davey's early years. But he spent as much of each summer as possible in Hueytown. The man who would later serve as general manager of Davey

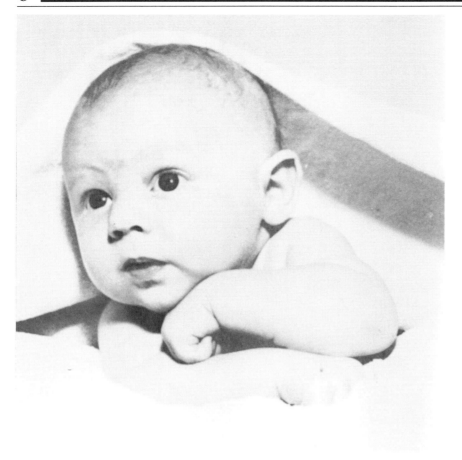

Photo courtesy of the Allison Family.

Davey Allison wasn't always a skinny kid, as this photo taken at about three months shows.

"Anything that had to do with racing, Davey wanted to play it. Davey and I had a race track we built around two houses. We raced around it on foot at first. My mother says now she has never seen kids run so much.

"We eventually moved up to bicycles, and we all had numbers. Of course, Davey was the same number as Bobby. He never cared much for getting beaten, I remember that. My dad still says Davey was the grittiest little boy he had ever seen. He always gave 110 percent."

Davey's preoccupation with racing often showed in his classwork, said Ellen McKinlay, Davey's third-grade teacher in 1969 at St. Aloysius Catholic School in Bessemer.

"Any teacher who taught him always said racing was all he thought about," she said. "Nearly all of his worksheets that he turned in had race cars drawn on them.

"We had trouble getting him to do his work. His was a bit of a daydreamer. He wouldn't want to complete his math or spelling, but Davey was smart. He had a high IQ."

At the end of each school year, teachers at St. Aloysius wrote notations about their students on the record cards. That way the teacher the following year would know what to expect. The notations on Davey's cards pretty much told his story.

A notation from his fourth-grade student card reads: "He thinks too much about racing." A note from his teacher on his fifth grade report reads: "He daydreams about racing in the classroom."

Bobby recalls Judy once having a discussion with a teacher regarding Davey's inability to conquer math.

"Judy told the teacher that if she'd let him add race cars instead of apples, she'd get his attention," Bobby said. "She tried it, and it worked."

Allison Racing said Davey was infatuated with racing as far back as he can remember.

"When we were 5 or 6 we had slot cars, and Davey was always Bobby Allison," he said. "There was nothing Davey ever wanted to be but a race driver.

"I remember that Davey had a bicycle race track around a couple of houses. He had a set of flags and everything. He'd get somebody to be the flagman, and he'd be out there racing four or five other kids on bicycles."

Lance Moore, now a Birmingham car salesman, lived one house away from the Allisons when they first moved to Hueytown. The same age as Davey, they became friends at 7.

"Davey was as normal of a kid as you'll ever find," Moore remembers. "He was all boy. A little mischievous, maybe.

Like most kids, he had some bad days, Bobby said.

"There were days I had to paddle Davey's backside," Bobby said, "but Davey was a really a good kid."

Those who remember the mischievous Davey may say now he was no Boy Scout. But in reality, he was. Davey and Clifford were members of Troop 207 in Hueytown from 1974 to 1976.

"That Davey was the cutest little devil you've ever seen when he was little," the Allisons' Scout leader Clarence Sellers said. "Davey was something.

"I remember we went to summer camp, and we were camped out near the chapel. We saw this big ol' hornets' nest hanging from a tree. I told the kids not to mess with it, but Davey and my son started throwing rocks at it. We were hollering that if they hit it not to come our way. Davey finally hit it and busted it open. I'll never forget that little fellow running through trees and bushes. He was scared to death."

Davey was the son of a famous man and became famous on his own. But he was never arrogant, Sellers said.

"Davey got along with everybody, and he was polite," he said. "He still called me Mr. Sellers to the day he died. Some people get famous and forget you. Davey didn't. He was always one of us."

Naomi Huddleston, a neighbor of the Allisons, remembers that Davey chose her backyard to launch his career as the next Evel Knievel. Davey was using a mound of dirt in her back yard as a ramp for his motorcycle.

Worried that he might injure himself, she told Davey that if he was going to jump in her backyard anymore he would have to cut her grass. She thought that would be the end of that.

Davey came back that afternoon with a lawnmower, cut her grass then went back home and got his motorcycle.

"No matter what Davey did you couldn't get mad at him," said Charles Wright, who watched Davey grow up during the years he worked for Bobby from 1970 to 1979. "Davey was something special."

Randy Hill met Davey on a playground at Pittman Junior High in 1976. Hill would eventually

Photo courtesy of the Allison Family

Even as early as age 8, Davey's school teachers said he daydreamed about car racing, sometimes to the detriment of classwork.

join Davey's crew as a member of the Peachfuzz Gang. Allison and Hill shared an apartment together for more than two years after they graduated from Hueytown High School in 1979.

"Davey was somewhat of a loner then," Hill remembers of his junior high days. "It wasn't because he was stuck up or rude - it was just because he thought about racing 24 hours a day.

"Davey didn't like school but he was a pretty good student, even though he never studied. He was a very smart individual. He didn't have to spend a lot of time in the books."

Moore said Davey had only one goal in life.

"Davey always wanted to be a race car driver when he grew up," Moore said. "Nobody ever forced him into it. That's just all he ever wanted to do. Davey paid his dues. He was dedicated.

"When his Dad told him that he couldn't race until he graduated, Davey went to summer school so

Bobby and Judy Allison pose with their four children for a photo published in the 1976 Birmingham International Raceway souvenir yearbook. The children from left are Clifford, Davey, Bonnie and Carrie.

he could graduate early.

"Four of us, including Davey, went to Panama City after graduation and we were going to stay 10 days. But Davey went home after four or five days so he could get back to work on his race car. That's how he was."

He and Allison double-dated some, but Allison was a lot more interested in race cars, Moore said.

"He didn't hang around much with anybody on the weekend," he said. "He was in that shop under a car."

Moore knew Davey for 25 years. In those 25 years he never changed, Moore said.

"Davey never acted like a superstar," said Moore. "All of his success never changed him. Anytime you were around him you were just around a friend. Davey liked everybody. Everybody had

their cliques in high school, but Davey fit in with everybody.

"I guess the most important thing you can say about Davey is that he never forgot where he came from."

Wright remembers that Davey always looked younger than his age. That, coupled with being Bobby's son, made him the target for a lot of good-natured kidding. It was always hard to pull the wool over his eyes, though.

"We were taking Bobby's short-track car to Boyd's Speedway in Chattanooga in 1976," Wright recalled. "It was cold in those mountains, and Davey never brought a coat anywhere. Everywhere you went somebody had to lend Davey a jacket. We stopped at a Holiday Inn, and John Smith let Davey borrow his jacket. John was a big man. Davey got out of the truck, and the sleeves of the jacket were dragging the ground.

"We were always picking at Davey. We got inside, and I winked at John and asked him if he'd been able to get off six weeks for the China trip. John went right along with me.

"I told him we had to have the car in San Francisco in two weeks, and it would take two weeks for the boat to get the car to China. Davey's eyes were getting bigger and bigger.

"I asked John what was the name of that town we were racing in and John named off the ungodliest Chinese name you ever heard of.

"Davey couldn't take it anymore. He said 'Y'all are pulling my leg.'

"I asked him: 'What makes you think we were pulling your leg?'

"He smiled and said: 'Cause my Mamma don't know nothing about it.'"

Davey was raised to respect his elders, and he never took the attitude that, "Hey, I'm Bobby Allison's son," Wright said. He said another incident with young Davey will always stick in his mind.

"Davey had just turned 16 and gotten his driver's license. So had Robert Brown, who hung around the

shop," Wright said. "Bobby was going to race in Pennsylvania, and I had to take the car up. Davey, Robert and I spent two days getting the car ready. Robert would say 'When it's my turn to drive the truck, I'm going to drive 70 mph.' Davey would have to outdo him and he'd say he was going to drive 80 when it was his turn.

"Bobby came by the morning we were leaving and asked me if I thought I could handle the two boys. I looked at both of them and asked them if

Photo courtesy of the Allison Family.

A bundled up Davey in the pits before the Daytona 500.

16-year-old Davey Allison worked the pit for his father, Bobby, in the 1977 World 600 at Charlotte.

they had enough money in their pockets to get back from anywhere we might be between here and Pennsylvania.

"They both looked confused. I told them that if I ever looked over at that speedometer and it was over 65 I was going to put whoever's butt was dri-

ving beside the road and let them get home the best they could.

"Davey looked at his Daddy and Bobby said: 'Son, I can't help you on this one.'

"Both kids drove the truck, and they both kept one eye on the road and one on the speedometer.

Neither one ever got over 65."

Davey was determined, even as a kid, said John Ozley, who worked for Bobby. He recalled an incident in 1976 that was evidence of that determination.

"Davey loved hunting," Ozley said. "Donnie had a hunting club down in Sumter County they called the 'Sumter Chateau.' A bunch of them went down, and Davey was going down the next morning.

"When he got up the next morning it had been snowing. Judy told Davey he wasn't going to get on those icy roads, at least not without snow chains. Davey went down to the shop and found a bunch of pieces of chains and some wire, and he wired them to his tires through the spokes on the wheels.

"He went up to house and showed Judy that he had gotten some chains, and she said OK.

"Of course, if Davey had gotten over 5 mph those chains would have fallen off. He got down the street, took the chains off and took off.

"That was how determined Davey was."

Tommy Allison spent many memorable moments with young Davey. He later became general manager of Davey Allison Racing Enterprises. He remembers that Davey could be a little mischievous at times.

"Davey was 17 and I was 15 and Bobby was having his engines built in Milwaukee," Tommy recalled with a laugh. "Bobby had this old Mazda pickup. He had an engine he needed delivered to

Birmingham News Photo

Davey always had that boyish look as evidenced by this 1981 photo when he was 20 years old.

Milwaukee and another engine he needed to be picked up. Davey and I took off up there.

"Davey had figured out that he could turn off the key of the truck and pump the gas and turn the key back on, and it would make a loud explosion.

"Anytime we saw somebody on the side of the road all the way up there and back he'd make that thing pop and he'd scare them to death.

"He came up on a bunch of hitchhikers and

pulled close to them. He made that thing explode, and they all dove in a ditch. We laughed about that for years."

Both he and Davey were able to live out a dream, he said.

"We used to sit on our grandmother's porch and dream about how someday we'd run this shop ourselves," he said. "In 1987, we made it happen. We've been living that dream every since.

"I wasn't ready for it to end, and I know he wasn't. But I consider myself lucky - and I know he did."

"Davey never acted like a superstar," said
Moore. "All of his success never
changed him. Anytime you were around
him you were just around a friend."

—*Lance Moore, boyhood friend*

"A lot of people think Davey had it made and had everything handed to him. The only thing Davey ever had given to him was opportunity. He took 110 percent advantage of it."

—*Tommy Allison*

Chapter Two

A Career Begins

If Davey Allison was destined to become a super-star, it surely wasn't evident in 1979. That's the year his longtime dreams of racing finally came true.

Cursed by big shoes to fill, no experience and a small racing budget, Davey's first season caused more than one pit wall analyst to declare that Davey was no Bobby Allison.

They would eventually have to eat those words.

Davey graduated from high school in January 1979, a full four months before the rest of his senior class. He had attended summer school in the summer of 1978 to get ahead. He went to work full time for Bobby Allison Racing and was given space for his own race car, but with the understanding that his job came first. He was allowed to work on his race car only after 5 p.m.

"We were building short track and sportsman (now Grand National) cars for Bobby, so there really wasn't time to build a car for Davey," said John Ozley, who worked for Bobby Allison Racing from 1974 through 1979. "Donnie had the shell of an old Nova he had raced a few years before, and he gave it to Davey.

"Bobby had the engine out of an old show car that had sat on an engine stand in the shop for more than a year. It had a lot of miles on it. He gave that engine to Davey to use. Bobby always contended that you learned to race with a car that didn't have a lot of power. You learned to race the car you had.

"Davey did a lot of the work on that car himself. I'll have to say for his experience and age, he put in a lot of work in that car."

On April 22, 1979, Davey's dreams of racing became a reality.

Davey, a few of Bobby's helpers and a group of 18- and 19-year olds - who would later become known as the Peachfuzz Gang - set off to conquer the world.

A beaming Davey Allison in the pits in Birmingham during his first racing season in 1979.

Birmingham News Photo

Young Davey Allison gets some advice from his father, Bobby, in 1981.

Davey's first race didn't have the storybook ending many would have liked to have seen. He worked his way up to third place before spinning out. He finished fifth.

"I was a little nervous," Davey said after that race. "I was running third and spun out. I guess I got a little nervous."

B.J. Parker, who operated BIR from 1977 to 1982, was a witness to Davey's first year of racing, just as he'd been for Bobby's initial racing season in Birmingham.

"Davey was just a little fellow," Parker said "Bobby made him do everything on his own. He wasn't well-financed like everybody thought he'd be. Davey worked with a lot of second-hand stuff.

"Davey would run near the front, but he wasn't

dominant. He didn't stand out like Bobby and Donnie did when they first came to Birmingham. Davey wrecked a lot.

"Part of the problem was the equipment he had. Davey didn't have any more than anyone else, and he had less than some. Bobby wanted Davey to learn about handling and making a car work instead of putting him out there with the fastest engine.

"Bobby and Donnie were a lot like Davey when they came to Birmingham. Everything they had was junk, too, but they'd outrun you with it."

Tommy Allison, Jr., was a member of the Peachfuzz Gang along with Kenny Allison (Donnie's son), Clifford Allison (Davey's brother), Mike Allison (Eddie's son), Randy Hill, Greg Campbell and Danny Defritas. Pop Allison was the pit boss.

"A lot of people think Davey had it made and had everything handed to him," said Tommy. "The only thing Davey ever had given to him was opportunity. He took 110 percent advantage of it."

Davey's first year of racing was a learning experience - an expensive learning experience, said John Smith, who worked for Bobby and helped Davey that first season.

"Davey tore up a lot of equipment," Smith said. "We had that Nova painted up blue and silver and all nice that first race, but we never bothered to paint it again the rest of the year. It was just primer from then on. We were too busy putting it back together to paint it.

"The first night we went to Montgomery Davey went down into the first turn and hit the end of the guardrail. I've never seen a car hit so hard. It just about tore the whole body off the car. It took two rolls of duct tape just to tape the sheet metal back on the car so we could get it back to Hueytown."

Smith said Davey's problem was obvious.

"Davey tried way too hard that first year," Smith said. "He thought he had to win. He'd been around Bobby and win, win, win all of his life. He thought he had to win, win, win.

"I had a talk with Bobby about it several times. Bobby would talk to Davey and tell him that if he was comfortable running seventh, then run seventh. But it wouldn't do any good.

"Davey won a race after about four weeks, but

Photo courtesy of Charles Wright.

Davey Allison (in car) puts on his helmet moments before his first race ever at Birmingham International Raceway. John Smith, foreground, and Charles Wright look on.

Davey Allison at speed in practice before his first race in 1979.

he didn't win many after that if I remember right.."

One incident especially sticks out in Smith's mind.

"We'd been working on the car all Saturday morning getting it ready to race in Montgomery that night," Smith said. "We got it finished, and Davey said he wanted to shake it down one time and then reset the alignment.

"I said 'That's great, but where do you think you're going to do that?'

"He said he was going to just run down the end of the street to the church and turn around and come back. He cranked it up and I heard him take off down the street. I heard him turn around at the church and he floored it again. Then everything got quiet.

"It was too far to walk down there, so I waited a few minutes. I finally decided that he probably stopped to talk to somebody. In a few minutes he cranked the car up again, and I heard him coming up the road. I went outside the shop and looked and the right front wheel was hanging . . . it was almost torn slap off.

"I asked him what happened and he said: 'You know that stump on the side of the road by the church? I met a car coming down the road and I guess I got over a little too far.'

"I think that was Davey's last time to test one on the street."

Red Farmer said Davey drove over his head that first year, but said that wasn't unusual.

"Every young driver is wild," he said. "It's natur-

Photo courtesy of the Allison Family.

Davey Allison's 1972 Nova didn't stay new and shiny long in 1979. After several accidents, the crew didn't bother to paint the car for the remainder of the year.

al to be overaggressive when you're young. They always drive more with their foot than their head.

"Plus, Davey was trying to impress Bobby. He wanted to do good because of his Daddy.

"But Davey had to work on his own car, so he wasn't as crash-bang as some of them. If he tore it up, he had to fix it. Davey didn't have anything handed to him.

"Davey could come to the shop and do anything to a car, including painting it. You could give him two pieces of angle iron and a cutting torch, and he could build a race car. Those kind make the best racing drivers."

Davey didn't always appreciate Bobby's way of doing things, Farmer said.

"It was that old thing about you're 16 and you can't believe how dumb your Daddy is. And when you get 21 you can't believe how much he learned in five years.

"He'd talk to me about Bobby, and he'd be ready to bite a broomstick in two. He didn't realize Bobby was doing things for his own good, but later he did."

Ozley remembers that Davey "had his spins and his share of crashes, but he adapted quick."

Did Ozley see a superstar in the making?

Ozley laughed.

"I saw a lot of desire," he said. "I thought he had the potential to be good. You have to remember that anytime you start racing...it's not an easy situation."

Randy Hill was a part of the Peachfuzz Gang,

but he insists it wasn't planned. He and Davey had been friends since junior high, but Hill had no desire to get involved in racing.

"I would come by the shop just to talk to Davey, and he started getting me to help with this and that," he said. "I remember he was taking an old Nova and stripping it down. I didn't know a whole lot about racing, and I wasn't a mechanic by any stretch of the imagination. I had rarely ever had a tool of any kind in my hands. I was a sports fanatic, but I never pictured myself as a race car mechanic.

"Bobby had seen me around the shop. One day Bobby got Davey off to the side and asked 'What's the deal with this guy?' Davey told him I was help-ing out. Bobby came over to me and told me that if I was going to hang around, I'd better keep up with my hours so they could pay me. I was hired."

Hill joined Davey's racing team shortly after Allison won his first race at BIR on May 5, 1979. He worked on Davey's team for three years. Shortly after joining Allison, they ventured out on their own for apartment life.

"My Dad had an apartment and was having to move. He said he would pay for the apartment for a while until Davey and I got going. I told Davey, and he said OK. He was ready to get out of the house."

Hill said he and Davey had very little social life in those days.

Photo courtesy of Charles Wright.

Davey's first crew in 1979 included (front row) left to right, Tommy Allison and Davey; (back row, left to right) Jake Allison, John Ozley, Pop Allison, Tommy Allison, Sr., and Charles Wright.

"We worked day and night. When we weren't working, we were on the road. We raced in Birmingham on Friday nights, in Montgomery on Saturday nights and somewhere on Sunday if we could find a race close by."

Davey was fortunate that first year because the frame under his car had been designed by his father, and the shop still had the jig the frame was built on, Smith said. "We'd always put it on that jig and somehow get it straightened out," Smith said.

Charles Wright was also a Bobby Allison Racing employee who pitched in to help Davey that first season. He remembers Davey's first win on May 5, 1979 well. It came less than two weeks after Davey's first race.

"Bobby got to the track just before the feature race the night Davey won his first race," Wright said. "They opened the gate and let Bobby across the track just before the race started. Bobby got to see him win his first race. I was always glad of that."

After winning, Davey came into the pits and looked "like a scared rabbit," Smith said.

Bobby made it an Allison sweep as he won the Winston 500 the following day.

Records show that after his first six feature races at BIR, Davey had one win, three second-place finishes, one third and one fifth. He eventually won a combination of four heat races and feature races at BIR that first year.

In 34 races at BIR, Montgomery, Dothan and Pensacola that year, Davey won five times and had 20 top 5 finishes and 29 top 10 finishes. He won $3,400 that first season.

"It's been a very exciting season," an 18-year-old Davey told The Birmingham News following the 1979 season. "I feel like I've learned a lot. The main thing I learned is that driving is a lot different than watching. You learn it isn't as easy to make those turns as it looks from the stands."

Hut Stricklin, who would later marry Donnie's daughter, Pam, was Davey's first big rival. He remembers those first years of racing fondly.

"I started racing a year before Davey did," he said. "And for the first year we raced it seemed like every time he'd get the lead I'd be running behind him, and he'd blow up one of those motors that he was building out of a junkyard.

"It got to where I'd win at Birmingham, and Davey would win at Montgomery. And then Davey would win at Birmingham, and I'd win at Montgomery. It was an ongoing thing."

Davey competed in the limited sportsman division again in 1980 and in 1981 moved up the NASCAR Grand American (now All-American) and All-Pro divisions. He saw limited success in the Grand American division and never won an All-Pro race.

He competed in the same divisions again in 1982 with limited success, and competed in a few ARCA events that year, too. He saw some action on the All-Pro and Daytona Dash circuits in 1983.

Davey's less-than-dominating efforts in his first few years of racing can be attributed to his equipment, Tommy said.

"Davey raced with hand-me-down stuff," he said. "Davey didn't win a lot of races, but he won a lot of respect. And he gained a lot of confidence."

John Smith remembers Davey's first big road trip which came in his second racing season.

"Bobby was in Daytona for the race. He called and told Davey they were having a big short track race in New Smyrna and that he ought to come on down," Smith said. "Davey was excited. Bobby told Davey he'd come out to the track and help him set up the car. Davey said he'd be there.

"We got down to Daytona and got a room on the fifth floor of this hotel. I woke up the next morning and tried to get Davey up. He'd mumble something and roll back over and sleep another 30 or 45 minutes. He was bad about that.

"I told him that Bobby was going to be at the track, and he was going to be mad because we weren't there. But Davey just went back to sleep.

"I went out on the balcony. I had some crackers and was feeding the seagulls. I said to myself, 'You know, I bet I can catch one of them things. I held a cracker up, and when a seagull came by I grabbed it.

"I went back in the room and pulled Davey's covers up. I threw the seagull in their with him. I don't have to tell what the seagull did.

"Davey jumped straight up in the bed. He was mad. He said he wasn't cleaning the mess up. I caught the seagull and let it go. I rolled up all the sheets and threw them in a corner. Davey was holler-

Photo courtesy of the Allison Family.

The Peachfuzz Gang, in 1981; (left to right) Kenny Allison, Tommy Allison, Danny Defritas, Greg Campbell, Mike Allison and Davey Allison.

ing the whole time that he'd get me back."

Davey got his revenge, Smith said.

"He didn't do anything for two months," he said. "He never mentioned it. But Davey knew how bad I hated snakes. Davey bought this big ol' rubber snake and waited one day until I was under the car working on it. He threw that snake under there with me and screamed 'Lookout John!' I saw what it was, and I almost tore all the skin off my head coming out from under there.

"I didn't think he'd ever quit laughing."

Bob Harmon, who operated Montgomery Raceway in Bobby's early Alabama racing days, is now the promoter for the All-Pro Racing circuit. In the early 1980s, that circuit boasted up-and-coming stars such as Rusty Wallace, Alan Kulwicki, Dick Trickle and Busch Grand National star Steve Grissom. Davey tried his hand on that circuit several times in 1982 and 1983, but could never win.

A 1983 race in Macon, Ga. still sticks in Harmon's mind.

"Davey showed up right before race time," Harmon said. "We didn't have an entry on him, and we didn't know he was coming.

"He didn't have enough money with him to register for the race, but they let him in anyway. Davey was always broke then. I used to think Bobby was too tough on him sometimes. But now I know why Bobby made Davey go through what he made him go through.

"Davey came up to me and said he wasn't supposed to be there. He said his Dad had gone to Pocono and told him not to take the race car out of the shop.

"About halfway through the 200-lap race, Davey wrecked. He totalled it . . . I mean he tore it all to hell. It took two wreckers to put it back on the trailer.

"Davey came up to me and said, 'I'm in trouble.' He wanted to know if I'd call his Dad and kind of pave the way for him.

"Davey dialed Bobby up in Pocono and handed

me the phone. Bobby said something like 'Bob, how are you doing? It's good to hear from you. Why are you calling me this time of night?'

Then it hit him.

"He said, "Is Davey there with you?'

"I said, 'yes.'

"Bobby asked, 'Has he got the Buick with him?'

"I said 'yes' again.

"Then Bobby said, 'He tore it up didn't he?'

"I said, 'Well, sorta.'

"He said, 'Tell Davey that I'm going to deal with him when I get home.'

"That night has been a big joke with Bobby and me ever since."

Those coming-of-age days were filled with pranks, broken cars, an occasional win, and experience-building situations.

But really, Parker said, Davey's first years of racing weren't very memorable, and he was never really competitive in racing until he reached the ARCA circuit.

Those ARCA days were just around the corner.

"I feel like I've learned a lot. The main thing I learned is that driving is a lot different than watching. You learn it isn't as easy to make those turns as it looks from the stands."

> —*Davey Allison at the conclusion of his first racing season*

"There was a caution flag, and the pace car pulled out in front of Davey. He radioed in and asked why they were putting the pace car in front of him. I had to tell him. I said Davey, I didn't want to tell you this, but you've been leading the race."

—*Randy Hill, describing a nervous Davey's first run on a superspeedway in 1980*

Chapter Three

The ARCA Years

Davey Allison's first victory on a superspeedway was on May 30, 1983. And true to the tradition of his father, he immediately began thinking about a short-track race.

Long after he became a star of the monster speedways, Bobby Allison continued to drive in relatively minor races on the bullrings. One writer likened it to a major league baseball player playing slow-pitch softball between games. "I race because I like to win," Bobby once said. "I race a lot because I like to win a lot." Of course, with his name and reputation he could command considerable show money.

Davey won the ARCA 500, a 500-kilometer event, at Talladega Superspeedway before 20,000 fans. After the victory lane ceremony and press conference he headed for Birmingham to compete in a Grand American event. "Every time I get in a race car I can learn something," he explained. "Besides, I'm racing for a living now."

Davey's first superspeedway victory came in a race marked by tragedy. Ken Kalla, a 35-year-old driver from Wheaton, Md., was killed when his car struck the inside guard rail on the backstretch on the third lap. He died of a "severe skull injury" after being taken to the infield care center.

The 22-year-old Allison won the Automobile Club of America event in a Pontiac after late malfunctions sidelined his two chief opponents, Ferrell Harris and Scott Stovall.

Harris was leading, with Davey on his bumper, when an oil leak sidelined Harris on the 95th lap of the 117-lap race. Stovall had closed to within 100 yards of Davey when his engine died on lap 112.

Davey's Pontiac finished more than a lap ahead of Marvin Smith's Oldsmobile. Curtis Payne was third in an Olds, Duane Pierson fourth in a Buick and Howard Payne fifth in a Pontiac.

Davey lifts the winner's trophy high after winning the 1983 ARCA 200 at Talladega.

Also in that race was veteran Hueytown driver and Allison family friend Red Farmer, who finished 14th after an oil seal fell out of his car in the late stages. Years before, Farmer had shooed Davey and his brother Clifford out of his shop when they would race through on their tricycles.

At the other end of the finishing order was another Alabama driver who frequently competed against Davey. Dave Mader III was relegated to last place when his car failed to get up to speed.

"This was the biggest race I've won, probably the most important of my career," Davey said.

Unanswered forever will be the question of what would have happened if Harris had stayed in the race.

"We'll never know," Davey said. "His car and mine were about equal in handling and horsepower."

Harris wasn't down-in-the-mouth, and perhaps he even realized he had been a player in a historic drama - the first superspeedway victory of a man who would become a star in their sport.

"It's hard to be badly disappointed because we ran so well," Harris said, "but we thought we had as good a chance to win as anybody.

"The car had been perfect all day. If the engine had lasted I don't know whether I would have won or not. I feel like I had the fastest car, but I don't know whether I would have won.

"It was a good race, and I'm sure Davey is excited. He has every reason to be. I know I'd be jumping up and down pretty hard if we had won. If you win at Talladega in any kind of race you've accomplished a lot."

Could Stovall have caught Davey if his car hadn't expired?

"I think I could have stayed far enough ahead of him that he couldn't have slingshot me," Davey said. "I could stay about a second ahead of him."

Watching from the pits was Davey's father, Bobby Allison. He talked to Davey on the radio. "He told me to use my best judgment about the lines I wanted to run and mash the gas," Davey said.

Davey's mother Judy and Bobby walked the 150 yards from the pit to victory lane side by side, proud parents.

"In victory lane he told me congratulations and that I did a super job," Davey said. "I don't know

what she said. Her smile was too wide."

Davey had little superspeedway experience when he won the ARCA 500 in 1983. His first run on a big track had been in an ARCA race at Michigan in 1980. In 1981 he raised eyebrows by starting ARCA's biggest race, at Daytona, in last place and finishing sixth.

Randy Hill was a member of the "Peachfuzz" gang in Davey's early years of racing. He said Davey's first trip to a super speedway at Michigan in 1980 was a memorable one.

"Bobby opened the window and hollered down at Davey and asked if if he wanted to run at Michigan," Hill remembers. "Davey said 'yes' and Bobby said to get the Matador in the shop. We all went crazy."

Hill said the Matador was an old car Bobby had raced. It had been used as a parts car and was totally stripped.

"It wasn't anything but a body and frame," Hill laughed. "We had two weeks to get it ready. I was 19 and the oldest one. We worked day and night to get the car ready.

"Bobby had a race somewhere else he had to go too, so Pop Allison kind of became the leader of the pack. This bunch of kids, who were way over their heads, took off to Michigan. Davey's grandfather and my Dad were the only adults that went."

That Michigan race will always be one of his fondest memories, Hill said.

"Davey blew the engine up in practice, and we all went to work putting in another engine," he said. "We didn't get the engine in in time for qualifying, but they let us start the race in last place.

"I guess I was the crew chief - if there was one - because I had the radios. The race started and Davey was so nervous I didn't talk to him. I just let him concentrate.

"Some guy - I forget who it was - just ran off and left everybody at the start. Davey slowly worked his way up from the back. The guy that was so far ahead had some kind of problems with his seat belts and had to come in. Davey didn't see him come in.

"There was a caution flag, and the pace car pulled out in front of Davey. He radioed in and asked why they were putting the pace car in front of him. I had to tell him. I said Davey, I didn't want to tell you this, but you've been leading the race.

"I'll never forget what he said - 'Oh, shit.' "

Allison was running in third place with just three laps to go when Bobby Allison's plane landed at the track. At the same moment there was a caution flag.

"I got on the radio and told Davey they were throwing the caution flag. He said, 'Yeah, I know. It's for me. I just blew up.' "

Davey scored the second of his four Talladega ARCA victories on July 30, 1983, giving him a season's sweep of the ARCA events at his home track.

This time it was his neighbor, Red Farmer, who came in second. The youngest member of the Alabama Gang beat the oldest by 75 yards.

Davey took the lead on the 34th lap of the 76-lap race and never relinquished it. He got a boost when Billie Harvey, who was a lap behind, passed him in the closing laps and Davey was able to draft Harvey and pull away.

"We had talked on the radio that he would be a good person to draft with," Davey said. "We knew we couldn't hold him back anyway. Thanks to Billie Harvey for coming up there and helping me get away from Red. If he hadn't, it would have been awfully close."

"We were right there at the end like we were supposed to be." Farmer said. "But Davey got hooked up in the draft and was able to pull away. And I had trouble getting around a lapped car, and that was all she wrote."

The race almost ended for him moments after it began. "Phil Barkdoll and Marvin Smith got together on the first lap," Davey said. "And I had to pass both of them while one was spinning and the other scraping the wall."

Farmer sat on the rear fender of his racer as his crew pushed it toward the garage, past victory lane where the winner was accepting his accolades.

"Way to go, Davey," Farmer said, though he couldn't be heard above the noise. "At least he kept it in the Alabama Gang."

"The car handled well all day," Davey said. "I couldn't have asked for better. It was good in the draft, good when I was leading."

Bobby Allison was in his son's pit, talking to him over the radio.

"He didn't tell me too much," Davey said. "He just mainly told me to keep an eye on lapped cars. Mostly he just asked me how the car felt, and I told him it felt good."

Referring to Davey's Talladega ARCA sweep, someone asked Bobby if he won two big races that early in his career.

"I may have won two heat races at old Dixie Speedway in Midfield," he said. "Nothing like this."

Davey was asked about having the example of his father constantly at hand. "There's no pressure being Bobby Allison's son," he said. "The pressure is that I want to win races."

He said his chances to win were better because he had started using his head as well as his foot.

"I was impatient," he said. "At first I ran wide open all the time. Now I realize you have to plan your moves."

The season of 1983 was delightful for the Allison family. Bobby finished ninth in the final event at Riverside to clinch the Winston Cup championship over Darrell Waltrip. Meanwhile, Davey won his first superspeedway race and added another big-track victory for good measure.

Davey also started his first Busch Grand National event, at Rockingham. He drove in just a few NASCAR Dash races, but he tied series champion Michael Waltrip for its Most Popular Driver award.

In 1984 Davey drove regularly on the ARCA circuit. He missed one event while he was on his honeymoon with his first wife, Deborah, and lost the championship by 25 points to Bob Dotter. However, he was named ARCA Rookie of the Year. He won ARCA superspeedway races at Atlanta and Talladega and a short-track event at Macon, Ga.

On March 17, a rainy-day crowd of just 5,000 saw Davey win the Georgia 150 at Atlanta. After the race, he announced he would run the entire schedule and try for the title. Previously, he had competed in occasional races for the Ohio-based sanctioning body.

"We talked about it in January, but put it on the back burner," he said. "Then after Daytona in February we talked about a way to build up my career. We couldn't afford to run NASCAR sportsman and thought the next best thing - maybe the best thing since they run on some superspeedways - was ARCA."

Davey dominated the Atlanta race, leading 97 of the 99 laps in his Pontiac. He earned $5,100. He beat Rick Wilson by a quarter mile.

Though his run to victory lane looked easy, it wasn't, Davey said. "The track got worse as the race went on. It got slicker, and the car got loose, and I had to take it easy. I slowed up two seconds a lap over what we qualified, just trying to keep the car straight."

Davey had appeared headed to victory in the ARCA 300 at Daytona in February, but a cut tire threw the win to Rick Wilson.

"I don't like to use the word revenge," Davey said, "but it sure felt good to know I was in front this time, especially after running as good as I did at Daytona."

Said Wilson: "Davey had more motor than we had. Our car was handling better than his was. But he was pulling me so much off the corner that I couldn't keep up. We lost an engine and had to change to a weaker one this morning."

The win at Atlanta tied Davey with retired Iggy Katona for the most career ARCA superspeedway victories. He would break the record if he could win the Permatex 500K at Talladega on May 5.

He did win, and in the process tied a mark held by Winston Cup driver Buddy Baker. They were the only men who had won three consecutive races at the world's biggest, fastest speedway.

Yellow was Davey's favorite color that day, and not because the jonquils were blooming. He had to have a yellow caution flag to win, and he got it.

Photo courtesy of the Allison Family, Photo by Chobatt

Davey poses with his Pontiac ARCA car at Daytona in 1983.

Davey and Wilson hooked up in a two-car draft and immediately left the rest of the contestants. They were nearly a half-lap ahead on lap 31 when a blown engine sidelined Wilson. Davey's Pontiac was in a class by itself after that, and he appeared headed to an easy victory.

But Wayne Peterson, Bill Scott and Mike Potter wrecked on the frontstretch, creating a caution period. The green waved on the 95th lap of the 117-lap race, and to the dismay of the 24,000 fans in the grandstands, Davey's car began to drop back.

He pitted with a flat right rear tire, apparently punctured by debris from the wreck. When Davey returned to the track, leader Duane Pierson was within 400 yards of lapping him. The only way Davey could catch back up was if there was another caution period.

Things got worse before they got better. A second tire, the right front, began going down. But on the 100th lap, Davey saw a welcomed sight - a caution flag produced by another car's tagging the wall.

Davey darted into the pits for fresh right-side tires. When the green waved on lap 106, his was the eighth car in line. But on the next lap he was in front and beat Pierson by 70 yards.

"I thought we were hung out to dry there for a while," Davey said. "We were lucky we caught the caution just right."

He almost lost control when the first tire went down. "All I could think of was to hang on. It was hairy there for a minute. The car got sideways, and I thought it was going to spin."

Davey's day almost ended in the first third of the race. He was in the pits when Connie Saylor lost control of his car and it spun, nearly hitting Davey's.

"I thought for a second we were out of the race," Davey said. "I saw everybody run from the right side of my car, and that made me look up at the mirror and I saw him. I don't know how he missed me."

Davey had won three Talladega races in a row. Could he make it four on July 28?

He won the pole, but neighbor Farmer won the race. "Well, at least we kept it in Hueytown," Davey said.

With Davey enjoying success, crowds at the preliminary ARCA events at Talladega were increasing. The May 4, 1985 Permatex 500 pulled 35,000 fans -

most of them probably his - and they weren't disappointed. He held off Lee Raymond and Farmer to win again.

Davey crossed the finish line 35 yards ahead of Raymond, and Farmer was on the runner-up's bumper. Raymond attempted a slingshot maneuver entering the third turn of the last lap. But he couldn't pass Davey, who stayed in the low groove.

Ken Ragan was leading the 500-kilometer race and Davey was just behind when Ragan crashed on the 108th lap of the 117-lapper. Davey barely missed being involved. Raymond spun but continued to race.

"There was oil all over the place, and Ken got sideways and hit the wall," Davey said. "My car went toward the wall, but I got it straightened out and went by him. I didn't touch the wall, but I came close."

Could Davey have beaten Ragan if he hadn't wrecked?

"Ken definitely had a very strong car," Davey said. "The only thing you can say is that I was sorry to see it happen, and I would have liked to have seen if I could have beaten him."

Did Davey plan to stay behind Ragan until he could try a last-lap slingshot?

"If Ken and I could have gotten away from everybody that's where I wanted to be," he explained. "But if we couldn't, I wanted to be out front because a lot of those guys, other than Red, don't have a lot of superspeedway experience, and they were running earlier like it was a short-track race."

Ragan and Davey had a half-lap lead when Ragan wrecked. The ensuing caution flag enabled Raymond and Farmer to catch up and make a race of it.

"I spun all the way down the backstretch and just grazed the wall on the right rear, but I never stopped," Raymond recalled of the accident. "When I turned around all I could see were race cars coming at me. I said, 'This is it.' "

He described his attempted slingshot: "On the last lap I was up under Davey on the backstretch, but there just wasn't enough room. He used up the whole race track. He's a smart kid."

Allison drove a Buick that had once been a

News staff photo by Steve Barnette

Davey in victory lane after winning the 1985 Permatex 500 at Talladega.

Pontiac. "We converted the car, and everybody was pretty run down and kind of skeptical," he said. "But all the hard work paid off."

Davey's final ARCA superspeedway victory came in the June 2, 1985, Georgia ARCA 500. It was stained by tragedy, just as his first ARCA super-speedway win at Talladega in 1983 had been. In each, a driver died.

Davey, driving a Buick, beat out Mike Alexander and Grant Adcox, the man who would succeed Davey as king of Talladega ARCA racing - and later lose his life in a crash at that very Atlanta track.

Stuart Lyndon died when a car he built himself rammed a dirt bank. The 35-year-old native of Hastings, New Zealand, "was self-employed, mostly doing body work, but he was a man obsessed by rac-ing," said his friend and crew chief Randy Jackson. "Every penny he had was in that car."

Davey won eight ARCA races in his career - four at Talladega, two at Atlanta and one each on short tracks at Macon and Indianapolis.

"…we talked about a way to build up my career. We couldn't afford to run NASCAR sportsman and thought the next best thing—maybe the best thing since they run on some superspeedways—was ARCA."

—*Davey Allison*

"I learned real quick that you don't just climb into one of these cars and go for 500 miles without being in shape. I'm going home and start working out."

—Davey Allison after
his first Winston Cup race

Chapter Four

On to the Big Leagues

Davey's Winston Cup career began on July 28, 1985, in the Talladega 500. He drove a Chevrolet owned by Hoss Ellington, for whom his uncle Donnie Allison had driven in the past. He finished 10th, two laps behind winner Cale Yarborough.

Bobby Allison had car trouble that day. But he was running at the finish and got 27th place, 46 laps down.

Davey was delighted as he exited Ellington's race car. "Well, we finished," he said. When someone told him he was 10th, he exclaimed, "That's great!"

But he was tired, too. "There's a heck of a lot of difference in running 500 miles as compared to 300 miles," he said, massaging his neck. "The longest race I had ever run before today was 312 miles. I'm happy to get the first one out of the way."

He admitted he was awed by his first entry into the big league.

"I sat there on pit road during the rain delay before the race, and I just kept looking at the other cars. I thought to myself, 'The numbers are all the same as the ones that I race against in any other race.' But then I looked at the sponsors and the colors. It hit me that the 22 car had Miller on it, and the 11 and 12 cars were sponsored by Budweiser, and the 33 car was the Skoal Bandit car.

"I thought, 'Here I am, going to race against the people that I was used to watching on television on Sunday afternoons.' I wanted to race, but I wanted to stay out of their way as much as I could and not be a problem for them on the track."

Ellington, who didn't field cars for the entire tour, was pleased. "He went real good, and I'm proud of the boy," he said. "As far as the traffic went he was careful, which was a good idea. At the end he was in the same lap with three or four other drivers, and he outran all but one of them. I was proud of

8	75	25.069	146.045
9	64	26.730	136.770
10	11	25.243	145.038
11	26	25.385	144.229
12	21	25.445	143.687
13	15	25.052	146.144
14	30	25.413	144.068
15	22	25.388	144.210
16	28	24.908	146.989m
17	46		(N.T.R.)

Davey points to his time and speed after winning the pole position for the Goodwrench 500 in 1987.

everything. The car's in one piece, and we ran all day."

Davey and his father drafted together for several laps during the race. "I really enjoyed being on the big track with Dad and racing against him," he said. "You know that he's out there somewhere, but when he's in sight he's just like any other driver you're trying to outrun.

"I knew Dad was having some problems during the race, and I hated that. Even though he was racing against me and I was against him, I still hated the fact he was not running well. He's still my Dad."

The major lesson he learned? "I learned real quick that you don't just climb into one of these cars and go for 500 miles without being in shape," he said. "I'm going home and start working out. It takes some kind of effort to muscle one of these cars for 500 miles. I promise you the next time I'm going to be ready - whenever next time is."

Next time was at Charlotte in October when Ellington's car blew an engine in the Miller High

Life 500. Davey got 19th place. His third and last start for Ellington was in the Atlanta Journal 500 in November. The engine erupted early, and Davey was relegated to last place. His Winston Cup earnings for the year totaled $11,715, tip money compared to the $1,955,628 he would earn in 1992. But he had his foot in the door.

Davey drove in four Winston Cup races for the low-budget Sadler Brothers team in the early part of the 1986 season without scoring a top-10 finish. His home track was kinder to him.

He competed in an ARCA race in May at the world's fastest speedway and finished second. Then, on July 27, he ran seventh in the Talladega 500 Winston Cup race. There is a story behind that one.

Davey's Hueytown neighbor Neil Bonnett, driver of Junior Johnson's Chevrolet, had been injured in a crash at Pocono the week before. He suffered, among other injuries, a fractured right shoulder and torn muscles and tendons in that shoulder.

On the day before the 500, Bonnett said: "I had

every intention of at least trying to start, but I've got only 20 percent mobility in my right arm. It would be foolish for me to start the race. I can't drive a passenger car, much less a race car."

So Bonnett went to the CBS booth to serve as color commentator for the telecast. Davey was named to drive for one of the most famous car owners in the game.

"Davey's an excellent driver," said Bonnett, who had never missed a race because of injury. "They've got a good chance to run up front and have a good finish."

"I'll just do the best that I can do," said Davey, who was without a regular Winston Cup ride. "The car was good in practice this morning. It was comfortable."

Davey started seventh, and Bobby started 21st. "I'm very glad he has the opportunity to drive in the Talladega 500, but I'm sorry it was at my best friend's expense," Bobby said.

Bobby Hillin won the race to become the youngest superspeedway victor in Winston Cup history. Davey stayed near the front all day, leading twice. He was in the lead dogfight at the end and finished seventh.

"He ran a good strong race, stayed out of trouble and brought the car home in one piece and in the lead pack," Johnson summed up.

Associated Press photo

Davey gets a few pointers from Bobby before the 1987 Budweiser 500.

News staff photo by Charles Nesbitt

Davey climbs from his Ford Thunderbird at Michigan International Speedway after winning the pole starting position for 400-mile NASCAR race.

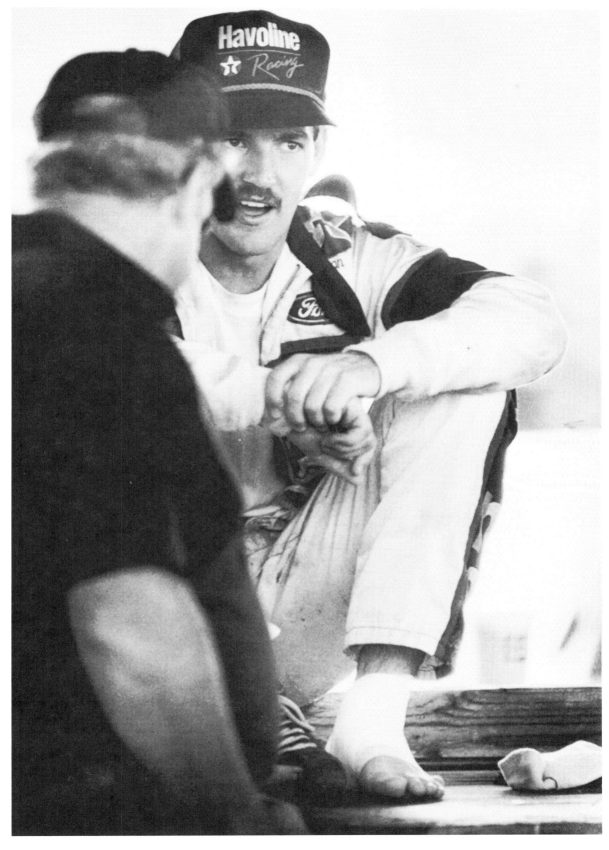

News staff photo by Charles Nesbitt

Davey Allison with burned foot after the July 1987 Talladega 500

Associated Press photo

Davey in the pits after claiming the pole position in the 1988 Winston 500.

"I was very pleased with his showing. Davey had a couple of tough breaks at the end of the race when the draft sort of fell apart, but that's part of racing experience. He'll get his share of that before he's through. His stock, as to getting a regular ride, definitely went up with a lot of people today."

Davey, who spent a sleepless Saturday night, was pleased with his showing. But there was some disappointment in his voice. "I guess I'm like every other driver, a little greedy when you don't win," he said.

His summation: "The car ran great, the crew did

a terrific job of getting me in and out of the pits, and I was fortunate to get through a couple of accidents late in the race that happened right in front of me.

"I really wanted to have a good showing today to help out Neil Bonnett. I never thought about proving anything to anybody by driving a strong car. I just wanted to do the best I could for Neil because of the faith that he had in my ability, which he showed by putting in a good word for me with Junior."

Winston Cup racing definitely was different than ARCA racing, Davey said. "The speeds weren't foreign to me, but in ARCA races you only have to race against five or six other drivers who run that fast. Today there were 40 cars that could run in that range, and that was a big difference. It was fun."

That race dramatically established that Davey Allison could take a top car and put it up front and contend for victory in the big league. But he didn't expect it to perform career miracles. He said he would continue to actively seek a top ride.

"Racing is a funny sport," he said. "A lot of drivers have been content to sit by the phone and wait on someone to call them. A lot of former drivers are still waiting.

"I guess that would be the easy thing to do, but one race doesn't make a lasting impression. I guess I'll be on the phone myself, calling around and working for a future ride. I don't want anybody to forget that I'm around and available."

Davey got his break. Ranier-Lundy Racing, a strong team that Bobby Allison had driven for, hired Davey.

Perhaps Ranier-Lundy's strongest asset was Robert Yates, a thoughtful son of a minister. Yates became manager of Ranier-Lundy in 1986. His reputation was that of a genius in the engine department.

Yates had prepared the engines for Bobby Allison's dream year, 1972. Driving for Junior Johnson's team, Bobby had raced to a phenomenal 24 top-three finishes in 31 races, winning 10 races and earning 11 pole positions.

He and Yates were together again in 1983 when Bobby won the Winston Cup championship driving for DiGard Racing.

Yates had noticed Davey back in 1984 when he

Birmingham News Photo

Mom and Pop Allison greet their grandson in victory lane following the 1989 Winston 500.

made an impressive - if unlicensed - practice run in his father's DiGard car.

"Davey drove our car at Charlotte for a couple of laps," Yates remembered the day after Davey's funeral. "Bobby was a little injured, and Donnie Allison had been driving the car some. I was clocking the cars and didn't know who was in it, but whoever it was was the fastest of anyone through the corners. It turned out to be Davey."

A NASCAR official "got him out of the car and chewed him out," Yates recalled. "He wasn't even eligible.

"That was my first observation that Davey was going to be a superstar."

Cale Yarborough, three-time national champion, had left Ranier-Lundy to form his own team. It was his huge shoes that Davey Allison was hired to fill.

The team considered several drivers, finally narrowing the choice to Rusty Wallace and Davey. Yates pointed out a couple of cold facts to Harry Ranier,

that Rusty had more experience and possibly could bring a sponsor to the team. "When he asked me about Davey I was very high on him," Yates recalled. "I had been around the Allisons, and they were a big part of my life, and I knew Davey could drive the car."

"Let's get Davey," Ranier said. Fine, Yates said.

His first race with Ranier-Lundy was the Daytona 500. Other sports hold their "Super Bowls" at the end of the season, but stock car racing opens its year with its biggest event. It was a load to put on the shoulders of a young driver who, since he hadn't driven in more than five Winston Cup races in a single season, was still eligible for Rookie of the Year honors.

Davey responded by qualifying second to Bill Elliott, the eventual race winner. His run of more than 209 mph made him the first rookie ever to start on the front row in the Daytona 500.

Then Murphy's Law did a remarkable number

on Davey and his team.

Davey was running with the leaders when he came in for his first pit stop. He returned to the track, and in the fourth turn a wheel fell off his Ford.

"We had a problem with the jack," Yates explained after the race. "It picked the front wheel up but not the back. The lug nuts were off the rear wheel, but we had to switch jacks. When we dropped the car to switch jacks, Davey thought that was the signal to go."

Alas, he went.

A pickup truck pushed his car back to the garage where having shredded lug nuts replaced ate up lap after lap. He returned to the race and finished 27th, 14 laps behind. As lawmaker Murphy says, whatever can go wrong . . . will.

Davey had his chin up. "Our jack broke," he said. "Somebody told me to go, so I took off with no lug nuts on the right rear. Seems like it took forever for the truck to get to me to push me back in.

"But I learned a lot here this week. The thing I really learned was that our Thunderbird was the car to beat. It ran and handled great all day long.

"We came in here and established ourselves as a contender, and people know that we're not any kind of fluke.

"We ran well all week long, and I know that this would have been our race if it weren't for the problems we had in the pits."

The Daytona 500 was two-thirds over when Davey shot by leader Dale Earnhardt. He steadily pulled away, putting five seconds between himself and the field.

There was one problem. He was 14 laps behind.

"We had the fastest car on the track today," Davey said. "I think that was shown once we got on our way after the problem in the pits.

"It's kinda frustrating because we wanted to prove we weren't here just to to make a quick splash.

"We were here to win. We didn't, and that's frustrating. But we can walk out of here with our heads up high and try to get ready for Rockingham.

"I feel like we got a victory of sorts, coming down here and having the car perform as well as it did."

In only his 10th Winston Cup race, Davey won

his first Winston Cup pole, leading qualifying for the Goodwrench 500 at Rockingham.

He finished ninth. He was 26th at Richmond, fifth at Atlanta and 27th at Darlington, the team passing up some short track races.

Then Davey Allison arrived in Talladega for the Winston 500. May 3, 1987, would be one of the most memorable days of his life.

"I was clocking the cars and didn't know who was in it, but whoever it was was the fastest of anyone through the corners. It turned out to be Davey.

"A NASCAR official got him out of the car and chewed him out. He wasn't even eligible.

"That was my first observation that Davey was going to be a superstar."

—*Robert Yates*

"I saw the fans in the grandstand waving me on. I couldn't hear them cheering, but I knew they were. It gave me cold chills."

—Davey Allison on his first
Winston Cup victory

Chapter Five

Davey Wins!

Little did the Allison family know that the 1987 Winston 500 would serve as a preview of the incredible highs and lows the family would endure over the next six years.

It was a day that began with Bobby's horrifying crash that narrowly avoided the unspeakable - putting a race car into the grandstands filled with people. It ended with Davey winning his first Winston Cup race.

When the traveling NASCAR show rolled into Talladega that week, the talk was about Dale Earnhardt and Bill Elliott, not the Allisons. Earnhardt had won four races in a row and six of the first eight races of the season. Elliott had put together a string of four consecutive Talladega pole positions.

Davey was considered among the few who had a legitimate chance to snap that streak. In February, Davey had become the first rookie to sit on the pole at Daytona. His qualifying speed of 209-plus putting him on the outside of the front row, next to Elliott. He also sat on the pole the following weekend at Rockingham.

It didn't take long for things to sour for Davey, however. He was taking his Ford Thunderbird for one last shakedown run on Thursday morning before qualifying. Coming out of turn four after having run a lap of 213 mph, there was a loud pop and the engine went silent. Back in the garage area, his crew opened the hood to find an expensive pile of broken and twisted steel.

"This leaves a big question mark," Davey said as he watched the crew remove the engine. "We'll just have to do the best we can. I think we could have run 213 or 214. I'm just glad it didn't happen in qualifying."

The crew, which included Davey's cousin Mike Allison, Greg Campbell and Andy Waldrop - all

News staff photo by Steve Barnette

Bobby Allison was involved in a terrifying crash early in the 1987 Winston 500. Davey went on to win that race for his first Winston Cup victory.

members of the "Peachfuzz Gang" that worked on Davey's cars in the BIR and Montgomery Speedway days - swapped engines in an hour and 10 minutes.

"That's getting with the program," Davey said.

It was then time for a high - actually two of them. Davey went out that afternoon and turned a lap of 210.610, which for a while had him on the pole. But not for long. Elliott eventually ran 212. 809. Then came Bobby, who qualified in his Buick at a surprising 211.809. Bobby's qualifing run upset the experts, who had predicted total Ford domination on qualifying day.

Davey had to settle for third and the inside second row, which wasn't bad considering he had qualified with a backup engine. The fact Bobby and Davy were starting second and third was a nice touch, though.

From top to bottom, it was the fastest field in NASCAR history.

"Not bad for an old man," Davey kidded Bobby, shaking his hand after qualifying.

"Just think how fast it would have run if you'd been in it," Bobby snapped back.

"Davey's been whipping me all year," Bobby said later. "It's nice to finally whip him."

The qualifying run had Bobby excited. It hadn't been a good year. He hadn't won a race since outdueling Dale Earnhardt at the wire in the Winston 500 the year before.

The Allison family joy continued Friday night as

Birmingham News Photo

Davey celebrates with crew chief Joey Knuckles after winning his first Winston Cup race in the Winston 500 at Talladega in 1987.

In the Victory Lane after the Winston 500 at Talladega in 1987.

up-and-coming 23-year-old driver Clifford Allison - Bobby's son and Davey's brother - won a 50-lap late model sportsman race at Birmingham Super Speedway.

The Allisons' jubilation didn't last long on race day. On lap 22 of the 188-lap event, Bobby ran over debris on the track and his right rear tire exploded as he exited the trioval. The car spun backward, became airborne and struck the fence that separates the track from the grandstands, narrowly missing the flagstand. It sprayed pieces of broken fence into the crowd like a shot from a shotgun.

Bobby's car rebounded onto the track and hit Cale Yarborough. Ron Bouchard, Alan Kulwicki, Darrell Waltrip, Mike Waltrip, Richard Petty and Benny Parsons were all caught in the crash. Bobby's car stopped in the middle of the track with the driver's door facing oncoming traffic.

The remainder of the field managed to miss Bobby's car.

The first rescue personnel on the scene said Bobby's first words were: "Are any spectators hurt?"

Unfortunately, there were injured spectators. All but one of the injuries were minor - one fan lost an eye because of the flying debris.

"I was listening to the radio on the radio headphone and they said something about Bobby Allison and something about trouble," one spectator said. "I looked up and he was in the fence in front of me. As soon as I saw the car in the fence and the fence rolling up I hit the ground."

Few were more terrified that Davey and Judy Allison.

"My heart sank," Davey said after the race. "I looked up the mirror and saw Dad against the fence. That was probably the lowest emotionally I'd ever been."

Davey said he prayed on the lap after the crash.

"I just asked the good Lord to let him stay on Earth with us a good long while," Davey said. "I came back by and saw him getting out of the car. That lifted my heart back where it should have been.

"It was definitely the worst crash I'd ever seen."

Judy Allison was also horrified as she witnessed the crash.

"Bobby's accident really looked bad," she said. "In fact, I thought it was going to be really bad. My first concern was to get down there and see if Bobby was moving around. When I got close I saw he was getting out of the car and I felt better - until I looked up in the stands."

Bobby's crash stopped the race for 2 hours and 38 minutes as crews repaired the frontstretch fence. Davey, Bobby, Judy and the remainder of the Allison family returned to their gathering spot in the infield to wait for the resumption of the race. Davey helped himself to a triple serving of ham and potato salad.

"I sure hope I'm able to get back in that seat, fasten the belts and finish the race after all I've eaten," he told the group.

Either a full belly or his father's wreck must have inspired Davey. When the race resumed, he punished the field for the remainder. Only a handful of caution flags kept the race close as the other drivers struggled to keep up with Davey.

The race was shortened 10 laps because of darkness and Davey took his first checkered flag in Winston Cup competition. He led 101 of the 178 laps.

"To get my first Winston Cup win at Talladega is fantastic," the rookie driver said afterward. "I saw the fans in the grandstand waving me on. I couldn't hear them cheering, but I knew they were. It gave me cold chills.

"The car was so strong all day I could do anything I wanted to. It handled so well it ran right on the bottom of the track. It's something to be able to do whatever you want to with a car on a track like this."

Davey's win was the first for a rookie since Bouchard won the 1981 Talladega 500.

No one was prouder than Bobby and Judy Allison following their son's win. They joined him in victory lane.

"It's been a weekend on the emotional roller coaster for sure," Bobby said after the race. "I know it's not the kind of ride I would like to go every weekend.

"Davey has worked awfully long and hard for this victory. He's paid his dues. He's worked with me and Donnie in the past and he's worked himself up the racing ladder, slowly but surely. His preparation has been excellent, and I'm as proud as I can be of him for what he's accomplished.

"It's been a day of tremendous emotions, with the wreck and now Davey's victory, but it's really great to end the day like this."

Mom shared Dad's pride.

"Proud. Ecstatic. Unbelievable," Judy Allison said. "I knew all along he was capable, but I really didn't think his first victory would come so soon. It's really two kinds of feelings when your husband wins and your son wins, and I really can't explain the difference, but they are both happy feelings."

Davey must have liked the taste of victory. He was in Victory Lane again just two races later at Dover, Delaware - making him the first rookie to ever win two races in the same season.

"I looked up in the mirror and saw Dad against the fence. That was probably the lowest emotionally I'd ever been."

—Davey Allison, describing his father's
spectacular crash in the 1987 Winston 500

"Give Davey two pieces of angle iron
and a torch, and he could build you a
race car."

*—Red Farmer, fellow race car driver
and Alabama Gang member*

Chapter Six

The Beat Goes On

Robert Yates was the ninth and youngest child of a prominent Southern Baptist minister with a large congregation in Charlotte. He was born in 1943, 19 minutes after his twin brother Richard, who is business manager for the team Robert owns, Robert Yates Racing.

He was the self-described "black sheep" of six girls and three boys.

When he was 12 he would get up at 3:30 in the morning and quietly push the family car out of the garage and down the street. When it was out of earshot of his parents, he'd start it and deliver his newspapers.

He would work. In fact, sometimes he'd work three shifts at Babe Maloy's drive-in as a cook and curbhop to buy car parts so he could drag race at Shuffletown Dragway.

In 1960 he attended the first World 600 at Charlotte Motor Speedway. That's for me, he thought, resolving to become part of the sport.

His preoccupation with things mechanical and his passion for street drag racing led to failing grades and a 13-month loss of his driving license in 1963. Black sheep, indeed; all his brothers and sisters were honor students.

But a sister who was attending Wake Forest Seminary and who would become a missionary offered to take Robert in for his final two years of high school. The effect of her influence was dramatic, for he went from a D average in Charlotte to straight A's his senior year at Wake Forest High School.

Robert even completed a two-year course at Wilson Tech and continued his education at Mars Hill College and Central Piedmont Community College.

Still, he loved the feel of a wrench in his hand more than the feel of a pencil. A professor saw him

Birmingham News Photo

Davey addresses the media, a common scene as wins begin to stack up and his fan popularity blossomed.

devour school books. Father Louis Giardino, pastor of St. Aloyisius Catholic Church in Bessemer, who delivered the eulogy at Davey's funeral, checked his school records and jotted down this judgment from the fourth grade: "He thinks too much about racing." And this ditto from the fifth grade: "He daydreams about racing in the classroom."

Both Allison and Yates were fascinated by the mechanical side of racing. "Give Davey two pieces of angle iron and a torch, and he could build you a race car," Red Farmer once said.

Farmer also ventured that if Davey had lived, he and Yates would have been together many years. "Davey wasn't the kind who up and changed teams if you didn't win a race," Farmer said. "Davey would have won the national championship, just like his father did, not this year but next year."

working on a tractor instead of studying for an exam and announced to the class: "There's one guy who's never going to make it. He'd rather be a mechanic."

He did become a mechanic. In 1968 he got into racing with the famed Holman-Moody Ford factory team, managing the air gauge department. His rise in the business was fast and dramatic, for he built the engine that LeeRoy Yarbrough drove to victory in the 1969 Daytona 500.

He built the engines that Bobby Allison used when he won 10 races for Junior Johnson in 1972. He built the engines that Bobby used in winning the 1983 national championship while driving for DiGard. He built the engine that Richard Petty used in scoring his historic 200th victory at Daytona in 1984.

Davey Allison and Robert Yates hit it off as driver and mechanic-car owner. Maybe because they were a lot alike.

Both were intelligent, but they hardly lived to

The day after Davey's funeral, Yates reflected: "Davey told me at Charlotte a few weeks ago, `Don't worry about anything. When I stop driving for you I'll hang my helmet up.'

"We were going to sign a contract for four years this week."

Yates continued: "I've never worked on a team that I got along with the driver as well as I got along with Davey. We never had one argument. It was so easy and so nice.

"Davey encouraged me to do things that were probably beyond what I thought I could do. He gave me confidence to do things I wouldn't have done on my own, and I hope I gave him confidence to do things he wouldn't have done on his own.

"He was a super guy to work with. But, then, I had a good relationship with the Allisons."

He recalled Bobby's being hired to drive for DiGard for the 1982 season. "In 1981 I asked Bobby to meet me in a church parking lot in Charlotte, and I talked to him about driving the DiGard car in 1982. He told me he wanted to. We won eight races that year, and in 1983 we won the championship.

`I did the engine for Davey when he won the Talladega ARCA race in 1983. I built engines for him later when he won ARCA races. I knew he was going to be good. His daddy raised him right."

Davey kept the crew pumped up, Yates said, never grousing when members made mistakes.

"One time at Daytona the car qualified third and was so fast - and it just cut off, and we didn't know why. We got it started, but then we had some chassis problem.

"Larry McReynolds, the crew chief, was to give him some information, and Larry said it in a discouraged voice. Davey said, `Now, that was wimpy.'

"It was like he was saying, `Come on, guys!'" When you wanted to run off and hide, he could get the team up."

Davey was the

Winston Cup Rookie of the Year in 1987. It was an honor his uncle Donnie Allison won in 1967. He set a record for rookie earnings with $361,060, though the team competed in just 22 of the 29 races. He won the Winston 500 at Talladega, and then his vic-

Associated Press Photo

Davey in garage area before 1989 Winston 500

Associated Press Photo

Davey climbs out of car after qualifying for the 1989 Winston 500.

tory in the Budweiser 500 at Dover on May 31 made him the only rookie ever to win twice.

"He was good, and our equipment was good," Yates said. "He would run the car as hard as the capability of the car, and that's hard to find. He had that background confidence from his father.

"The Ford wasn't a good race car in 1986, but it came back to be a good car in 1987. And we got Texaco, which was important."

The driver of the Texaco/Havoline Ford Thunderbird rejoiced after winning at Dover. "I could get used to this," Davey said.

He and his father dominated the race, which was run in heat that topped 90 degrees. Bobby led 147 of the 362 laps, but his Buick overheated.

"I hated to see him fall out," Davey said, "but I think he would have taken second anyway."

Bobby had won seven times at Dover, but this Bud was for Davey. "I was really happy with the car today," Bobby said, "but I think a piece of paper or

something got on the grille, and before I could get the car in it overheated and cracked the block."

Davey had an anxious moment when, with 17 laps to go, he overshot a pit stop, barely avoiding the pit wall. But he kept his cool and circled back around and got a squirt of fuel and beat Bill Elliott by nearly seven seconds. He averaged 112.952 mph and earned $46,600.

"I did all I could do, and that was it, period," said Elliott. "We came and ran and finished, and I don't feel bad about that."

The Monster Mile, as the Dover track is called, was a worthy opponent. Only 20 cars finished.

The 1987 season was a rookie-year dream. Davey won five poles, and three times he was the No. 2 qualifier, giving him eight front-row starts. He won two races and narrowly missed three more victories, finishing second by margins of one second, two seconds and 15/100ths of a second.

"We had an excellent car on some occasions, but

Davey was the guy who got the most out of it," said Yates. "We were miserable at North Wilkesboro. We were miserable at a lot of short tracks."

The 1988 season began with a memorable Daytona 500. Bobby won, and Davey finished second, on his bumper. Their Hueytown neighbor Neil Bonnett was fourth.

Bobby led the final 18 laps, Davey unable to perform a slingshot at the end. It was the first father-son 1-2 finish since Lee and Richard Petty took the top two spots in a 100-miler at Heidelberg Speedway near Pittsburgh July 10, 1960.

"It was really good to be in front," Bobby said. "It was a great feeling to look back and see somebody you think is the best driver coming up and know it's your son. It's a very special feeling, and it's hard to put into words."

That race will be remembered for another episode. Richard Petty's car did a horrifying dance on the frontstretch, disintegrating and tearing down part of the catch fence after a brush with another racer. Fans feared the sport's No. 1 winner might be dead, but he escaped without serious injury.

Yates reflected on the circumstances of that historic 1988 Daytona 500 as they involved his team.

"We were on the outside pole and we wrecked the car in the last five minutes of practice," he recalled.

The team could use that car or bring in a back-up racer and start at the back of the field. The crew members rolled up their sleeves.

"We didn't want to give up the front-row starting position, so we worked on it all night long," Yates said. "We had to put everything in it.

"Davey got in that car and ran second place to his dad. It wasn't hard to take second place to his dad. It's always good to run in the top five at Daytona. It was like a storybook, and I was glad to be part of it.

"Davey followed Bobby's tire tracks and Bobby's footsteps. That car is in the International Motorsports Hall of Fame's museum at Talladega, and it will always be a neat memory of mine."

One of the spectators was wife and mother Judy Allison. She was delighted with the success of her men - but she was practical. "I was pulling for Bobby," she said.

Why?

"I knew him first."

The Hueytown housewife smiled and added: "And he still pays the bills."

She called it her biggest day in racing, and she hugged them both. It was a nerve-wracking race and a nerve-wracking ending for Judy. "I was biting my nails without biting my nails," she said. "I was hoping nothing would happen. I've seen so much happen on that last lap."

It was a nice Valentine's Day present, watching her husband earn $202,940 and her son earn $113,760.

"It's got to be neat for both of them," Judy said. "You think about a finish like that happening some day, but when it really happens you don't believe it."

Davey was smiling. "I feel pretty good," he said, "especially after getting involved in an accident yesterday and getting the car put together last night."

Daytona 500 finishes can get nasty, but neither Bobby nor Davey considered the possibility this time.

"I've seen over the years how fair he is," Davey said. "I knew if I had the car to beat him, I'd beat him, and he wouldn't do anything out of the way."

Said Bobby: "I've always played it straight, and when I'm racing against the best youngster to come along, I wouldn't do anything different."

Davey drafted on Bobby's bumper much of the day, but he said it wasn't prearranged. "I'll work with anybody out there that works with me," Davey said, "and Dad was the only guy out there that would work with me today."

Reporters kidded Bobby about winning the sport's biggest race at age 50. "What it proves, maybe, is that I'm a late bloomer," Bobby joked.

"What it proves," Davey interrupted, "is that he's a winner."

The 1988 season, which began on such an upbeat note, turned into horror when, on June 19, Bobby Allison was grievously injured in a crash in the Miller High Life 500 at Pocono. He hasn't raced since, except in an exhibition.

"Davey always drove with all he had," Yates said, "but it was like that gave him an even greater desire to get it done."

Davey won two races that year, the Aug. 21

Champion Spark Plug 400 at Michigan and the Sept. 11 Miller 400 at Richmond.

Davey drove a masterful race to beat Rusty Wallace by 4.43 seconds at Michigan after going winless in the season's first 18 events. There were just two caution flags, and Davey's average speed of 156.863 miles an hour was a record for the track.

Davey had trouble containing the tears when he went to victory lane before 72,000 fans. "I dedicate this race to my father, my family, and all those loyal race fans who are the reason we keep racing every week," he said.

"We've had every type problem you can think of this year. Not just engine problems; we've had tire problems, driver problems, dodging wrecks and causing wrecks.

"Today I had all kinds of thoughts going through my head. Between my father and friends of mine like Neil Bonnett and Harry Gant getting hurt and everyone talking to me about this darn sophomore jinx, it hasn't been much of a year. I'm just as a happy as I-don't-know-what to win. The sophomore jinx is dead."

Davey took the lead for good on lap 178 of the 200-lap race, passing Wallace and extending his lead.

Davey earned $57,800 for winning Richmond and set a track record for the fewest races required to reach the $1 million in Winston Cup purses. In 52 events he had made $1,052,785. The record had belonged to Dale Earnhardt, who in 1981 reached $1 million in his 76th race.

But something happened that day that couldn't be measured in money.

Just before race time, the public address announcer at Richmond International Raceway told the crowd of 60,000 that a special guest would give the ceremonial command to the gentlemen to start their engines.

The next voice, transmitted through a telephone hookup from Alabama, was that of Bobby Allison.

"I was kinda prepared for it," Davey said, "so it didn't catch me off guard as bad as it might have, but it still sent cold chills down my spine."

He added: "I don't think anyone realizes how much I miss him."

Davey led 262 of the race's 400 laps and pulled

away late to beat Dale Earnhardt by 3.25 seconds. He averaged 95.770 mph in the first race at the new D-shaped .75-mile Richmond International Raceway.

On Oct. 1, 1988, the team became Robert Yates Racing. The man the professor thought would never make it because he wanted to be a mechanic had bought his own Winston Cup outfit from Harry Ranier. Davey earned $844,532 that season.

It was a time of change in stock car racing when the carnival-colored machines lined up for the 1989 Daytona 500. Cale Yarborough, Benny Parsons, Buddy Baker and Bobby Allison weren't there.

Yarborough and Parsons had retired and Baker had been forced to the sidelines by crash injuries, though he would drive occasionally after that. Richard Petty, once the king of the Daytona 500, no longer was competitive, and he barely made the field. Later in the season, David Pearson officially retired after he made a practice run at Charlotte and decided he wasn't up to 500 miles. He hadn't raced in three years anyway.

Those six had won 513 Winston Cup races— virtually a third of the 1,548 that had ever been run.

But the sport was in good hands with such relatively young but seasoned drivers as Davey Allison, Kyle Petty, Dale Earnhardt, Bill Elliott, Alan Kulwicki, Mark Martin, Ricky Rudd and Ken Schrader in the cockpits.

Davey didn't win the Daytona 500, but folks who don't remember who did win it (Darrell Waltrip) remember a move Davey made.

Geoff Bodine's car clipped Davey's early in the race, sending it into a long slide on the backstretch. It hit a dirt embankment and turned completely over, coming to rest on its wheels. Davey continued to drive the Thunderbird and finished 25th, seven laps behind.

"That's the kind of guy Davey was," Yates reflected. "He didn't see a car flipping over as a reason not to go on."

Yates remembers 1989 as "the year we were trying to get the car handling good and trying some engine stuff. We didn't have our act together, but Davey was never discouraged. He kept me pumped up. He said, 'You'll get it. You'll get it."

Davey won the Winston 500 at Talladega on May 7, 1989. A crowd of 140,000 saw him hold off Terry Labonte in one of those patented last-lap Talladega thrillers.

"This is my home track," Davey said. "All my family and my friends are here, not to mention that we've won some races at this speedway.

"We needed to focus on Talladega, and we did. For instance, in our testing we spent an entire day working on the qualifying setup. We had never done that before, anywhere."

The focus paid off. Davey, who started on the outside front row, beat Labonte by 22/100ths of a second.

Davey's car was the strongest in the pack, for it led 94 of the 188 laps, but he had to work for the victory.

Morgan Shepherd was leading, and Davey was second when a multi-car crash on lap 172 brought out the caution flag. The green waved on lap 177, and the last chase of the day was on.

Davey dogged Shepherd and finally got around him on lap 180. Davey, Labonte and Mark Martin linked up in a three-car duel.

Labonte tried to pass on the frontstretch dogleg on the last lap, but he found Ernie Irvan's lapped car there. He moved high, but he didn't have the juice to pass.

Was Davey certain he had the power to hold off Labonte?

"I didn't know whether I had the power or not," he answered, "but I made sure I was in the place they wanted to be in.

News staff photo by Bernard Troncale

Davey and crew chief Larry McReynolds tried to figure out what went wrong after qualifying went poorly in the 1991 Talladega 500.

"I wasn't going to do anything stupid, but I was sure going to protect that lead."

Where did he expect Labonte to make his move?

"Anywhere," Davey responded. "I don't think I looked out the windshield the whole last lap. I know this place by heart, so I can drive it with the rearview mirror.

"If they were going to make a move anywhere on the track there were going to be three cars going that way, not two."

Labonte said he did all he could do. "I think Davey was holding back today. We couldn't do anything with him. Mark Martin couldn't do anything with me, and I couldn't do anything with Davey. It was a good run for us, though."

Said pole-sitter Martin: "We weren't strong enough. We were there, but we didn't have anything for Davey at the end.

"Terry and I were doing this and that, trying to get something up," he explained, demonstrating hand signals, "but when the time came we couldn't even get up to Davey. The way Davey was running, nobody was going to beat him."

Davey averaged 155.869 mph and earned $98,675. And his father watched from one of the speedway's VIP suites.

"I can't wait to see him," Davey said. "This is the first race he's been to since he was injured at Pocono that we won. He's been to several, but not that we won."

In fact, the audience was liberally sprinkled with members of the huge Allison clan. Talladega is home.

"This has been an up and down season," Davey said, "but this is the best place to turn it around."

He was well armed for the turnaround. "This was a grand race car," Davey said. "It drove perfect. All I had to do was steer it and mash the gas."

The win snapped 14-race winless string. "I just wondered if we were ever going to do it," Yates said. "It's good to get the first win of a season."

Now Davey had won four ARCA races and two Winston Cup events at Talladega. Someone asked him to reveal his special knack for getting around the huge track.

"If I knew the answer to that question I wouldn't tell anybody," he answered.

Davey's first victory at Daytona, the mecca of stock car racing, came on July 1, 1989, when he won the Pepsi 400. His parents viewed the race from one of the speedway's suites and then headed for a half-mile track at New Smyrna Beach to watch younger son Clifford compete in an All Pro event.

Someone mentioned that Bobby battled the 2.5-mile course on many afternoons before he finally won a Winston Cup race there, the 1978 Daytona 500.

Davey's reply was perfect: "Well, they say it's easier to find a place if somebody shows you the way. I had an advantage because I had followed him down pit road to victory lane before."

He was referring to their thrilling 1-2 finish in the 1988 Daytona 500.

The first thing Davey did when the victory lane ceremony was over was go to his parents and say, "Thank you for everything."

"What a thrill!" the recuperating Bobby said of his son's victory. "When you come back from a deal like I did, this makes it even better."

He continued: "It's hard to compare this to anything else but Davey's winning at Talladega earlier this year. I had a real nervous afternoon watching that one. I almost chewed my fingernails off to the second joint.

"Judy told me, `You see now what you've been doing to us all these years.' "

It was a strange race for Davey. He clearly had the strongest car in the field, but he led only 19 of the 160 laps, and he didn't take the lead for good until the 155th lap.

Circumstances kept knocking him into bad track position—and he kept charging back toward the front. At the end he edged Morgan Shepherd's racer by two car lengths.

During a caution period that started on the 23rd lap, Davey had to make an extra pit stop while his crew replaced the ignition system. He returned to the track at the rear of the field, but without the aid of a drafting partner he passed car after car, and within 20 laps he had caught the lead draft.

During a yellow period that began on the 47th lap, he again had to pit twice, this time to correct a tire problem. Again he went to the back of the pack, and again he charged up through the field.

With 40 laps to go, Mark Martin and Davey were pulling away from the rest. Davey was drafting Martin to conserve fuel.

The caution waved on lap 131, and Davey pitted for gas and right-side tires. The other frontrunners gambled and maintained their positions. When the green flag was displayed on lap 134, Davey was 10th - not as far back as he had been during the other two crises, but at a definite disadvantage.

Once again he picked off his competitors, car by car. He caught the lead pack of five on lap 136, and the question was whether he could pass five strong cars in 24 laps.

His chances weren't improved by two more caution periods that took away six of the 24.

But the race finally went under green for good on the 149th lap. Ellliott, Martin, Allison, Shepherd and Phil Parsons motored away.

Martin was leading with six laps to go when he ran out of gas and lost a lap. Davey shot by him and held off Shepherd for the victory.

"I had the upper hand once the race got going," Davey said in the postrace press conference, "but during the week we didn't. We made some adjustments yesterday that helped.

"It was scary being back in the pack, but fortunately we worked our way back up to the front before anything happened."

Shepherd said he didn't realize the last lap was the last lap, and that may have cost him the victory.

"I had a shot at it," he said. "I could have won it. I missed seeing the white flag. Davey could pull me down the back straight, but if I could have just gotten my nose underneath him in turn three it would have been just like putting on his brakes. I missed the opportunity. That was going to be my last-lap move."

Davey didn't believe Shepherd could have taken him. "Morgan was awful strong," he said, "but I tried to make him and Mark Martin think they could beat me in a couple

Davey extends his fist in victory after capturing the Banquet Frozen Foods 300 at San Jose, California's Sears Point International Raceway in 1991.

of places where they really couldn't have."

Sacrificing track position for tires and fuel late in the race was "a gamble that paid off," Davey said. "Our Thunderbird was getting loose, and we needed tires. I told the crew it was too loose, and I didn't want to take a chance of somebody getting up under the rear bumper and turning us around."

Would his fuel supply have allowed him to finish without that final stop?

"Part of our strategy was to draft Mark Martin and conserve fuel," Davey said. "I think we would have made it to the start-finish line and then probably run out immediately."

If Martin had won he would have earned a $100,000 bonus. The money was posted for any driver who could win both the pole and the race.

"I don't have much to say about the gas situation because the gas is not my deal," Martin said, meaning calculating fuel was the crew's responsibility. "My deal is to drive the car and get everything out of it that there can possibly be. I did that."

For the second year Davey had run the entire schedule, but he finished 11th in 1989, compared to eighth in 1988, and his 1989 earnings of $640,956 were less than 1988's $844,532.

The team hoped for better in 1990 as he again took on the full circuit, but he finished 13th in the standings and won $640,684. For the third straight season, he went to two victory lanes.

"It was still a searching kind of year," Yates said. "We were trying to get the handle back on the car, and we were trying some new engine pieces. Toward the end of the year we started to get what we were looking for."

Davey did win his first race at one of the traditional short tracks. On April 9, 1990, he took the Valleydale 500 at the .533-mile Bristol International Raceway. He had won at the new .75-mile Richmond track in 1988, of course, but it's neither fish nor fowl, being longer than a short track and shorter than a superspeedway.

Davey gambled and won the Valleydale 500 by an official distance of six inches over Mark Martin.

He stayed on the track when the leaders made a pit stop during the final caution period on lap 392. He advanced from eighth place to first and stayed there the rest of the 500-lap race.

Davey called his staying on the track while the others pitted a team decision.

"We elected on that last caution to gamble," he said. "I kinda felt like it'd go the rest of the way under green. And we also knew that our car would be better on those tires that had some laps. We needed to stay out, so we gambled as a team. And it paid off."

On the last turn of the last lap, Martin got in the low groove and pulled up beside Davey, and that's how they ran the final 175 yards to the finish line.

"I knew if I stayed in my line it would be tough for him to pass," Davey said. "He got a real good run off the fourth corner, and I didn't. I think I was trying to protect my line more than get to the checkered flag.

"I almost let him get by me. But I did what I had to do. I didn't cut him off. I gave him racing room, and we beat him."

Davey said he knew he had won the photo finish. "I knew I was ahead of him when we crossed the stripe, but it didn't really sink in until we came around. I was coming down the back straightaway, and I said, `Man, we just won this thing! I cannot believe it!' I started screaming on the radio."

It was the second straight runnerup finish for Martin. "Boy, we got close," he said. "It was a great run for us. We did all we could do, but there just wasn't enough race track to get by Davey. We had a great car, but we just didn't quite make it to the front. I gave it a shot there at the end. We were just six inches short, I guess."

A track-record crowd of 57,800 saw Davey average 87.250 mph.

Davey didn't win again for six months. He took the Mello Yello 500 at Charlotte on Oct. 7, 1990. "It's been a long time coming," he said. "It's been a trying time for the team. Fortunately everyone stuck together, and it paid off."

Bill Elliott was dominating the 334-lap race until the 258th circuit when an equalized tire forced the first of three unscheduled pit stops. He had led 243 laps, once building a runaway advantage of nine seconds. He finished 15th, three laps down.

"There's not much to say except this is the way

Associated Press Photo

Davey relaxes in the Grand National garage on Friday between practice runs at the Alabama International Motor Speedway before competing in the Talladega DieHard 500 the next day.

the whole season has been going," Elliott commented. "Davey was good, but I don't think he could
have beat us. But that's racing."

Davey took command after Elliott's problems
and led 57 of the final 76 laps, including the last 12.
He held off Morgan Shepherd and won by 3.4 seconds. He averaged 137.428 mph enroute to the winner's purse of $90,650.

"Bill is probably the only other guy who's had as
bad a season this year as I've had," Davey said. "He's
sitting there with one victory. Before today I was in
the same shoes. But Bill's a tough competitor, and
he'll be back."

The Allisons thus became the first family to pro-
duce three race winners at Charlotte. Father Bobby
and Uncle Donnie also visited victory lane in
Winston Cup racing's hub city.

"I was pulling for Bobby. I knew him
first. And he still pays the bills."

—Judy Allison, following the 1988 Daytona 500
when Bobby and Davey finished one-two

"I feel like I'm sitting here with the best youngster there is out there, and he happens to be my son. I'm very, very proud. A lot of fathers around the country would like to feel this way about their son."

—Bobby Allison, upon Davey's
1992 Daytona 500 victory

Chapter Seven

Seasons in the Sun

Davey Allisons's rookie season of 1987 signaled that the team had marvelous potential. But over the next three years the great promise remained just that - great promise. Davey won two races in each of the four seasons.

Then came 1991 and a dramatic surge into the rarefied atmosphere of Winston Cup excellence.

"From 1988 through 1990 we just flattened out," Davey said, but he called the '91 season "the first one where we made significant improvement. It was the most incredible season I ever dreamed of."

In 1992 the team proved it was no one-year wonder by again cutting a broad swath through Winston Cup - though 1992 also would be remembered as one of the most punishing years in Davey's life, as he suffered injury and the death of his grandfather and brother.

In 1991, Davey:

Won five races, plus The Winston, the sport's all-star event, earned $1,732,924, finished third in points standings, and led more races (23), more times (73) for more miles (1,879.12) than any other driver.

In 1992, Davey:

Won five races, plus The Winston, earned $1,955,628, finished third in points standings, led more laps (1,362), more miles (2,315), more times (tied at 50) than any other driver and scored the most top-five finishes (17).

Yet, after the first four events of 1991, who would have predicted such a marvelous season for Robert Yates' team? Davey finished 15th, 12th, 16th and 40th. He found himself in 21st place in the standings. If he could have erased those first four

Davey talks with crew member during 1991 DieHard 500 qualifying

races, he would have been the champion.

After those four disasters, Yates hired Larry McReynolds as crew chief. According to Davey, McReynolds was the ingredient that enabled the team to soar.

"His personality and style fit our team perfectly," Davey said. "Communications between Larry and me are better than with anybody I ever worked for. And he communicates with the guys in the shop. He makes them want to do it rather than feeling they have to.

"We had been trying to get Larry for two years. Robert asked me who I wanted, and I told him if I could have anybody on the circuit, I'd pick Larry.

"It's like putting a 500-piece jigsaw puzzle together. It's not complete until that last piece is in. Larry was the piece that completed our puzzle."

McReynolds, 33, is from Birmingham. His beginnings in racing hardly indicated he would be voted Winston Cup's Mechanic of the Year in 1991 and Crew Chief of the Year in 1992. He started as a volunteer on a street stocker driven by his aunt, Noreen Mears, in 1975.

McReynolds worked at a junkyard. He helped prepare cars for such short-track hotshots as Richard Orton, Dave Mader and Mike Alexander. He broke into Winston Cup in 1980 by answering an ad in a NASCAR publication. He was hired as a full-time crewman on Bob Rogers' team.

He became a Winston Cup crew chief in 1986 when Kenny Bernstein hired him for his new team. Joe Ruttman, Morgan Shepherd, Ricky Rudd and Brett Bodine drove Bernstein-McReynolds cars before McReynolds moved to Yates' team in 1991.

In his first race with McReynolds, at Darlington, Davey finished second. He was off and winning.

On May 19, 1991, Davey won The Winston at Charlotte. It didn't count as an official victory, but the grocery store didn't quibble over whether the $325,000 purse he won was legal tender.

The Winston frequently is a wild affair, but this one bordered on boring. Davey started on the pole and led the 70-lap event from flag to flag. "This was so easy it was scary," he said.

Davey brought up some history. "Rusty Wallace and Bill Elliott each won The Winston prior to winning the Winston Cup championship," he said. "That's one of our goals. I feel this is a strong step in that direction.

"When you can win against the best in the business, it's going to build your confidence up."

Davey beat Darrell Waltrip in the opening 50-lap segment. Then he outdistanced Ken Schrader by 2.87 seconds in the 20-lap finale.

"The biggest thing about starting from the pole is that you can dictate what you want to do," he said. "There's a lot of money at stake. When you're out front you feel like you won't get caught up in any of the action."

His defeated opponents were impressed.

"Davey looked stout, and he'll come back strong next week for the Coca Cola 600," Dale Earnhardt said. "We'll just go to work and bring another car back for next week and see if we've got anything for him. No one had anything for him today."

"I don't know what he's got, but he's got something - or they've all got it," Waltrip said of Davey and the Fords. "I don't know which. But he's certainly showing it. We couldn't even hardly stay with him on restarts."

"If we had gone longer, Davey would have just been further ahead," said Schrader.

Birmingham News Photo

Davey pauses during qualifying before 1991 DieHard 500.

Earnhardt was correct when he said Davey would come back strong in Charlotte's Coca-Cola 600. He led 264 of the 400 laps in NASCAR's longest race, beating Schrader by 1.2 seconds. He stayed strong, turning the race's fastest lap, 168.329, five laps from the end.

Earnhardt, who finished third, decided the winning team was cheating. "Ain't no way you can outrun an illegal race car," he said.

Responded Davey after scoring Ford's first

points-race victory of the season: "He's a guy whose won two races this year. Now I've won one and my car's illegal. Something's funny about that."

Grousing about NASCAR's allowing the Fords extra lift on the rear end didn't set well with Davey. "I'm a driver," he said. "I don't make the rules. They made it possible for us to raise the rear deck up. It increases the downforce on the back of the car, but it doesn't make it go faster. If they want to point fingers, well, how many races has Chevrolet won this year and how many has Ford won?"

After the race, Davey could beam: "The thing ran flawless all day. Everything they did to the car made it a little bit better."

But the day didn't begin well for him. His car was the last one pushed to the grid. Leaking valve seals were discovered when the crew fired up the car that morning.

"I came in, and I didn't really feel good," Davey said. "I had been sick in my stomach and didn't sleep good. I walked over by the car, and they were taking the engine out of it. I thought I was going to throw up on the spot.

"They said the engine they were putting in was a twin to the one they were taking out. I felt a little better, but we were nervous about what was going to happen."

A crowd of 160,000 saw Davey earn $137,000 to go with the $325,000 he picked up for winning The Winston eight days before.

"These times don't come very often," he said. "We savor them while they're here. It felt so good to know I could pass on the inside or the outside, on the straightaways or the corners."

Birmingham News Photo

Discussions in the pits were frequent before big races.

Davey scored his first road-course victory June 9, 1993, at Sonoma, Calif. It was a controversial win.

Davey was leading on the last turn of the 73rd lap of the 74-lap event when Ricky Rudd's car hit his from the rear, bumping it aside. Rudd drove on to apparent victory with Davey second, four seconds behind.

But NASCAR imposed a five-second penalty on Rudd so that he would finish second, the position in which he had been running when the bump occurred. Davey was declared the winner.

"The last four or five laps everybdy was racing hard," Rudd protested. "It was an accident. I got into Davey."

"If the roles would have been reversed it wouldn't have happened," Davey said, "because I would have raced him clean. I'm not saying he did it on purpose, but I think it could have been avoided."

Rudd professed to being dumbfounded by the decision. "It wasn't an intentional type of rub or hit or trying to take anybody out. We got together. I've never experienced anything like this. This wasn't even to the point where we got to racing each other and rooting and gouging. This was just a racing accident."

Waddell Wilson, manager of Rudd's team, said: "I think we officially won the race, and we played by NASCAR's rules to do it. We were trying to pass the car, not spin it out."

Les Richter, NASCAR's vice president for competition, viewed video tapes and made the decision. He said the bump was a flagrant violation.

"It would have been more difficult to judge if Ricky had been on the quarterpanel of Allison's car," he said. "It wasn't. He hit Davey in the rear end and spun Davey out. He was running very hard into the corner, racing hard to win. But there comes a time when you have to call balls and strikes, to make a judgment call."

Asked if the controversial finish detracted from his victory, Davey replied: "Does my smile look any smaller?"

Davey won the Miller 400 at Michigan on June 23, 1991. Hut Stricklin, driver for Bobby Allison's team, finished second. Stricklin was an old friend of Davey and is married to his cousin, Pam Allison.

The victory was a replay of his runaways in The Winston and the Coca-Cola 600. A crowd of just under 100,000 saw Davey lead 107 of the 200 laps and win by 11.7 seconds. He drove the same Thunderbird that buried the competition at

Davey keeps an eye on the action during qualifying for the Talladega 500 in 1991; with Sterling Marlin of Columbia, Tennessee, left, and Rick Mast of Rockbridge Baths, Virginia.

Davey signs an autograph for an admiring fan at the 1991 Buckmasters Classic.

Charlotte.

Bobby Allison watched the race with mixed emotions. "We're looking forward to the day when we can get our Buick in front of that darned old Ford of Davey Allison," he said. "Really, this outcome today is a neat deal.

"Davey has been a lot of pleasure to me along the way, and I've talked to Hut about that. I told him on account of that I just want him to beat Davey by a little bit - but I do want him to beat him."

"It was great to see Hut behind us," Davey said. "I congratulate Hut and the guys on Dad's team. They're coming on.

"We are, too, which I guess is pretty obvious since we've won three of the last five races. We've been hung up on winning two races a year, so to finally get a third one in the same season is real sweet."

Several opposing crewmen said that on the night

before they feared Davey would be untouchable, and he was. "The car drove perfect, like it was on rails," he said. "My only concern was that a smoking car near the end of the race might cause a caution flag, which would've allowed the others to close up on me. That can lead to anything happening. Thank goodness they didn't have to throw the yellow flag."

Said Stricklin: "Davey and I have been friends since we were kids. We came up through the short-track ranks together. But the next race I want it to be a 1-2 finish for us, the other way around."

Davey's victory in the AC Delco 500 at Rockingham on Oct. 20, 1991, came despite the domination of Harry Gant.

Gant led 260 of the 492 laps and at one point, after lapping most of the field, had a seven-second lead. But a 30-second pit stop 40 laps from the end decked him.

Davey took advantage of the slow stop to beat Gant by a second and score his fourth win of the season.

"We thought we had them whipped there at the end," Gant said, "but our strategy went a little wacky. We came into the pits eight seconds ahead of Davey and were going to take on tires and gas. But then the air wrench broke, and we ended up coming out eight seconds behind him. That's where we lost the race."

The 51-year-old Gant was bidding for his fifth victory in a seven-race span. Earlier in the season he had won four straight, tying him for the modern record. He led huge chunks of the Rockingham race that included 84, 56, 49 and 53 laps.

Davey was confused by Gant's long stop until he heard from his crew. "I didn't know what had happened," he said. "I thought he was coming out ahead of us. The guys told me on the radio he had a bad stop and we were leading the race. I was a little nervous because I thought Harry had had a great stop and gone out ahead of us.

"I'll tell you what, I kept looking up in my mirror and seeing that old man coming. I was sweating."

With two races left, Davey trailed defending champion Dale Earnhardt by a virtually insurmountable 203 points and Ricky Rudd by 43. His poor finishes in those first four races had ruined his chances to win the Winston Cup title.

"I never look back and think about what might have been," Davey said. "I look back and say I'm glad what happened is over with and look forward to the future. I think we have the best shot at a Winston Cup title next year."

Davey won the next race, too, the Pyroil 500 at Phoenix, on Nov. 3, 1991. But Earnhardt won the war. Earnhardt finished ninth, and that meant he had only to start the final event of the season, in Atlanta, to be the champion.

Earnhardt, the fierce competitor, wasn't totally pleased, though. "We didn't have it today," he said. "The motor was a little weak, and the chassis setup was a little bit off, too. I wish we could have been a lot better here. I would have liked to have wrapped it up here. But if I don't fall out of a tree deer hunting

Birmingham News Photo

Davey leads Ernie Irvin during 1992 DieHard 500.

Associated Press Photo

Davey lifts his arms in the air after winning the Daytona 500 in February, 1992, at Daytona Beach, Florida.

shocks, a sway bar, the wedge and lamber and the panhard bar.

"We made so many changes this morning, if somebody had been in there watching us they'd probably have thought we were crazy," Davey said. "And they'd be right. But it worked."

Off-season speculation had Davey as the driver most likely to unseat Earnhardt from the Winston Cup throne in 1992. He wouldn't hang himself with optimistic pedictions, though.

"I don't make predictions," he said. "The only thing I'll say is that I'm more anxious than I've ever been."

He did, however, admit: "I feel 1992 will be our best chance ever to win a Winston Cup championship."

Asked to compare the 1992 model Davey Allison with the 1987 Rookie of the Year, he answered:

"I'm not going to say I'm a better or worse driver. I've grown up a lot, and I'm more patient. I don't punch trailers any more." Angry at losing at Talladega the year before, he slugged his car carrier with his fist and broke his hand.

Veteran Darrell Waltrip believed Davey made considerable progress as a driver in 1991, that he "grew into" a very powerful race car as the season went on.

in the next two weeks we'll be OK."

Davey rolled to a convincing victory, finishing 11.41 seconds ahead of Darrell Waltrip.

"As far off as we were in practice Saturday, to be so good today, I just can't believe it," Davey said. "I sat down last night and talked to Larry McReynolds and Donnie Allison, and we decided to try some things today."

He said his team changed two springs, two

"The car demonstrated more than once that it was superior to any on the race track," Waltrip said. "I've been impressed by the car - but sometimes we overlook the fact that somebody has to steer it around the track."

The optimism of Davey's fans doubled when he won the opening race, the Daytona 500, on Feb. 17, 1992. He reached victory lane of the sport's Super

Associated Press Photo

Davey talks on his headset at the Charlotte Motor Speedway as he prepares for the Coca-Cola 600.

Bowl by surging past a mid-race crash that damaged 14 cars, including those of a half-dozen leading contenders.

Davey dominated the last half of the race, leading 98 of the final 102 laps, and beat Morgan Shepherd by two car lengths to earn $244,050.

The pivotal wreck occurred on lap 93 when Ernie Irvan drove under the leading cars of Sterling Marlin and Bill Elliott, creating a three-abreast situation heading down the backstretch.

Here's how Marlin described it: "Bill was coming down, Ernie was coming up. I thought, 'This ain't going to work.'

"I got sandwiched. We were all hung together, and I thought we were going to shake loose. Then it turned me across the track."

Irvan commented: "I'm sure there was a way I could have kept it from happening. But I'm sure

Sterling and Bill could have avoided it, too."

Davey was running just behind those three in fourth place when the crackup began.

"There was no question in my mind," he declared. "That was not going to work. I knew it. I went the other way and got the heck out of there.

"I saw Sterling jump under Bill Elliott and Ernie Irvan follow him. I followed Ernie at first until he pulled down under Sterling and made it three-wide coming out of turn two.

"I said, 'Whoa, this is enough for me. I'm backing off.'

"They just ran out of room. They all got together. When they did, I moved to the outside, stood on the gas and went on.

"I looked in the mirror, and all hell broke loose right behind me."

The three wrecking cars ignited a demolition

that benched Marlin, Rusty Wallace, Ken Schrader, Chad Little and Dale Jarrett. Damage to their cars killed the chances of Elliott, Irvan, Dale Earnhardt, Darrell Waltrip and Mark Martin.

"It took out all the people who had a shot at it except Davey and Morgan Shepherd," said Martin. "I'm going to tell you right now, we had a car that could've put on a show. So did Elliott, and so did Sterling."

Davey set the pace after the crash, but Shepherd hung on gamely. He just wasn't strong enough to pass.

Shepherd's chances all but died when he lost his drafting partner, Michael Waltrip, whose engine failed with eight laps to go.

"I'd have had to have some help from behind to draft by Davey," Shepherd said. "He was stronger than us. I could get a run at him, but it wasn't quite enough."

Said Davey of the closing stages: "I was very concerned. I spent 90 percent of each lap looking in the mirror, trying to figure out which way Morgan was going to go.

"I knew he'd have a tough time getting around me on the outside. Anytime either of us went up high, on either end of the race track, it really bogged the car down.

"We had to run in the bottom lane to keep the speed up. So I knew if I could stay at the bottom and stay in front of him on the straightaway, he was going to have an awful tough time getting around me. Stay in the way - that's the only strategy I had."

Davey said some of the cars involved in the wreck could have made trouble for him. "Sterling Marlin and Bill Elliott were about equal to us. Then Dale Earnhardt's and Ernie Irvan's cars were both strong. If they hadn't gotten torn up they'd have been a factor, too, at the end of the race. A lot of things fell into place, but that's the way this business goes sometimes."

Davey wrecked his primary racer in a Wednesday practice and drove a backup car in the

Associated Press Photo

Davey talks with crewman as he prepares for another race on the Winston Cup circuit.

Birmingham News Photo

Davey and his wife, Liz, in a 1992 photo

500. "I'm not so sure we didn't run the best car we had," he noted.

All's well that ends well. "I was probably the most dejected person in the whole garage area for doing something as silly as what I did in practice," Davey said. "I felt embarrassed. All night Wednesday I tossed and turned and couldn't get a good night's sleep, thinking I'd ruined my chances at the Daytona 500."

He wouldn't call his 1992 Daytona 500 victory the greatest thing that ever happened to him. In fact, he mentioned finishing second to his father in the 1988 Daytona 500. "That day was such a special day," Davey said. "I don't think anything will ever replace it."

He reflected on being the son of Bobby Allison: "I never had a burden on my shoulders because of my Dad's name. That's the greatest advantage a kid

like me could ask for.

"I don't want to be as good as my father. I want to be as good as Davey Allison can be. Whether that's better than him or not as good, I don't think it matters as long as I do the best job I can.

"That's one of the things I learned from him. He didn't measure himself up to somebody else. I'm not going to measure myself up to somebody else."

Bobby Allison won the Daytona 500 three times. "I feel like I'm sitting here with the best youngster there is out there," he said after joining the 1992 winner, "and he happens to be my son. I'm very, very proud. A lot of fathers around the country would like to feel this way about their son."

On April 1, Ed "Pop" Allison, Bobby's father, the patriarch of the Peachfuzz Gang, died. Four days later Davey crashed at Bristol. It was with separated cartilage, fractured ribs, a bruised lung and torn ligaments and muscles in his right shoulder that Davey returned home for his grandfather's funeral.

Because of Davey's injuries, Jimmy Hensley practiced and qualified the car at North Wilkesboro. But Davey, equipped with a quarterback's flak jacket and a special seat to relieve pain, drove in and won the April 12, 1992, First Union 400.

He dedicated the victory to his grandfather.

"I'm feeling pretty good right now," Davey said when he crawled into the car to start the race, "but there's no telling just how long this is going to last. Jimmy will take over when it gets too bad for me."

Hensley had a long wait, for Davey never gave up the cockpit, though he said he thought about it "1,000 times."

He won a furious late battle with Rusty Wallace - and the race.

"All I was trying to do was start the race, run a few laps and see how I felt," Davey said when it was over. "Well, once we got going I forgot everything else except trying to get back to the front. And then all I could think about was trying to win the race.

"I'm sure I won't feel quite this good in the next couple of days, but right now I'm standing here in a little bit of shock after this victory."

That season of ups and downs turned downward on April 26 when Davey hit the wall at Martinsville, reinjuring his ribs.

But on May 3, 1992, he led 110 of 188 laps to win the Winston 500 before the homefolks at Talladega.

That meant he was eligible for the Winston Million, a $1 million bonus posted by R.J. Reynolds for any driver who could win three of the circuit's Big Four races - the Daytona 500, the Winston 500, Charlotte's Coca-Cola 600 and Darlington's Mountain Dew Southern 500.

"I really don't want to think about the Winston Million too much," he said, "because I think that might take away from what our real goal is. The Big Apple is what we want, and that's at the end of the

Davey proclaims Al Unser No. 1 after the 1993 IROC race at Talladega.

Fans crowd along the rail to see the number 28 car roar past.

season." The Winston Cup champion's trophy is annually presented in New York, and the win at Talladega gave Davey a 67-point lead over Earnhardt at the top of the standings.

In the Winston 500, Davey won a last-lap shootout over a pack that included Bill Elliott, Dale Earnhardt, Sterling Marlin, Morgan Shepherd and Ernie Irvan. Elliott got second, finishing door to door with Earnhardt. There were two lengths beind Davey.

Davey credited a fine tire built by Goodyear and "the calls Larry McReynolds made on pit road during our two final stops" with his victory. The two factors were related, he said. Because the tire worked so well, McReynolds called for fuel only during the last two stops. "Track position was critical, just as it always is at Talladega," Davey said. "Being in the front of that train was much better than trying to win from second or third or fourth."

On May 16, 1992, Davey captured the historic first nighttime event at Charlotte Motor Speedway. He won The Winston, NASCAR's all-star race, for the second straight year.

He and Kyle Petty roared to the finish line side by side. They tangled, and after he had won, Davey's car crashed into the outside wall, driver's side first.

Davey suffered a concussion, a bruised lung and bruised legs, but was released from the hospital the next day.

In his hospital room, an IV in his arm and his wife Liz asleep in a chair, Davey grinned and said, "This is some victory lane, isn't it?"

"Davey was pretty shook up and confused when he got to the hospital," Yates said. "He was out for a little while. His eyes kind of rolled back a couple of times, but he came around. He's determined to run the Coca-Cola 600. He's a tough customer and has a lot of stamina. I think that's the character from his Dad."

Birmingham News Photo

Davey always took time to sign an autograph for every fan.

Davey could have won the Winston Million with a victory in the 600 eight days after The Winston, but he finished fourth and Earnhardt won to break a 13-race victory streak for Ford.

"We had to fight the car all day," Davey said. "We were good for short periods of time, but the chassis setup just seemed to fade away a little bit. It's a new car, and a fourth-place finish isn't that bad at all. We gave it our best shot."

On June 21, 1992, Davey led 160 of 200 laps and won the Miller 400 at Michigan. For the second straight Father's Day, he had given Bobby a win at Michigan.

"This could not get old," Bobby said. "I guess we'd like to try and make a routine of this."

It was a routine 3.31-second triumph over Darrell Waltrip.

"Something tells me Davey was on cruise control," Waltrip said. "If we gained, he gained."

"In the early stages of the race there were some cars that were pretty tough," Davey said, "but it seemed like the further we ran the better we got, and we could start to get away from the rest of those guys.

"For the last 30 laps Robert and Larry screamed at me to save fuel, save fuel, save fuel. And that's pretty much what I did."

Davey spent a couple of nights in a hospital for a virus, but he won the pole for the July 19, 1992, Miller Genuine Draft 500 at Pocono.

He had led 115 laps when, with just 50 laps to go, the left rear of his car and the right front of Waltrip's touched, sending Davey's Ford into a spectacular 11-flip crash. Waltrip went to victory lane. Davey went to the hospital.

That night, surgeons installed two plates in Davey's broken forearm and pins in his dislocated, shattered wrist. He also suffered a broken collarbone and severe swelling and bruising of his face and head. For the first time that year he trailed in the point standings - by 19 to Elliott.

In a memorable show of courage, Davey started the DieHard 500 at Talladega the next Sunday. A brief rain shower brought out the caution. On the fifth lap, Davey turned the car over to Bobby Hillin, who had qualified it third. Hillin finished third to put Davey back in the lead in point standings.

Two weeks later, road racer Dorsey Shroeder drove in relief for Davey at Watkins Glen. The team finished 20th, and Elliott was atop the standings by 17 points over Davey.

On Aug. 13, Davey's younger brother Clifford was practicing in a Grand National car at Michigan. He crashed and was killed.

The next day, tough-minded, tough-bodied Davey Allison qualified third for the Champion Spark Plug 400 at Michigan. On Aug. 16, he gutted out a fifth-place finish in his first complete race since the crash at Pocono.

He went to Darlington for the Southern 500

with a chance to win the Winston Million. He led 72 laps and was in excellent position to claim the prize. But just after he pitted for fuel, rain cut the race short, handed the victory to Waltrip and relegated Davey to fifth place.

Despite the pain, breakage and heartache, Davey wasn't done winning in 1992. On Nov. 1, he took the Pyroil 500 at Phoenix and returned to the top of the points standings.

"It's been a real up-and-down year, a great season and a bad season all in one," he said. "There are some people I wish were here to help us celebrate who can't be here."

He spoke of his grandfather and his brother. "I wish they could have been here," he said. But his voice started breaking, and after a long pause he sat up straight, smiled and said: "Enough bad stuff. Let's talk about the good stuff."

He led Alan Kulwicki by 30 points and Elliott by 40 with only the Hooters 500 at Atlanta on Nov. 15 remaining. Lee and Richard Petty were the only father-son duo to win the Winston Cup title. Davey could cause the Allison name to accompany that of Petty by finishing fifth, or by finishing sixth and leading a lap at Atlanta.

"Let's talk about that after it happens," he said with a grin.

"We'll just go and do the best we can, and the cards are going to fall were they're going to fall," Kulwicki said. "Today is another good example. You can never tell what's going happen."

Luck was riding with Davey. Pole winner Rusty Wallace led 161 of the first 203 laps before a dead battery, of all things, put him out of contention. Mark Martin had a five-second lead over Davey in the late stages. He pitted under green, and then a spinout by Jeff Davis let Davey pit under yellow and take the lead. Davey beat Martin by 3.19 seconds.

Elliott, who was leading in points at the start of the race, nursed his sick-engined Junior Johnson Ford to 31st place.

"I just didn't believe it could happen," Davey said. "Bill and Junior and those guys are just too

Photo Birmingham News

consistent."

Davey said he felt for Martin, and he hated to see other drivers have problems, "but we've earned where we are right now."

The Hooters 500 was a dream race for the promoters. It not only featured the points showdown featuring Davey, Kulwicki and Elliott, it was the last race in the distinguished career of Richard Petty.

When it was over, a hard-working Yankee with Mighty Mouse embroidered on the front of his uniform was the champion. Alan Kulwicki finished second in the 500 and won the title, Elliott finished first, and Davey finished 27th.

Davey was running sixth on lap 253 of the 328-lap race when Ernie Irvan's car spun and crashed into his. Davey returned after 45 laps of repairs.

"The guys deserve better," Davey said, referring to the crew. "They made a gallant effort. They earned the right to be champions. It just wasn't meant to be. I hate that our race came to an end the way it did."

He placed no blame on Irvan. "It looked like Ernie must have had a flat tire or something," Davey said. "The car just got away from him."

Kulwicki finished with 4,078 points, Elliott with 4,068 and Davey with 4,015.

Who could have dreamed that Kulwicki and Davey both would die in aircraft accidents the next summer?

So the season of dreams and nightmares ended for Davey Allison. He embarked on 1993 with a positive attitude, and his chin up, the way he approached most challenges in life.

He finished 28th at Daytona and 14th at Rockingham, but he clung to the "we'll get 'em next week" outlook - and he did get 'em the next week, winning the Pontiac 400 at Richmond.

Davey led 152 of the final 157 laps and finished 20 car lengths ahead of Rusty Wallace.

"You just can't believe what was going through my mind and the pressure these guys have had on them after the first two races," he said. "This is exactly what we needed."

It was Davey Allison's last victory.

"It's been a real up-and-down year, a great season and a bad season all in one. There are some people I wish were here to help us celebrate who can't be here."

—Davey Allison at the conclusion of the 1992 season

"The past three years he made over 100 appearances a year for Texaco and Ford. A lot of those were two-hour autograph sessions that stretched into three- and four-hour sessions. Davey wouldn't leave anyone without an autograph."

—*Tommy Allison*

Chapter Eight

Davey, Off Track

She sat in the back of a pickup truck, her red hair shining in the South Carolina sunshine.

What good ol' Southern boy could have resisted hitting the brakes?

Elizabeth Mayson was at a charity autograph session near Darlington that fateful summer day of 1988 - not as a racing fan, which she wasn't, but as the guest of a friend whose husband owned a local race track.

It would be a day that changed the 22-year-old commercial real estate salesperson's life.

"Davey's really shy so this is kind of strange," she said. "When he came up, I was sitting in the back of a truck. He jumped up and said, 'What's your name?'

"I thought, 'Oh, my goodness, who is this?'

"It was 100 degrees, and he had on corduroy pants and a long-sleeved shirt.

"Now, I knew something about racing. I knew who Richard Petty was. Everybody does. But I didn't know who Davey was.

"After he walked off, my friends told me that was Davey Allison.

"He was very unlike what I had been attracted to before. But we got to be good friends and to know each other well. After we started seeing each other, I knew that was the man I was going to marry."

Davey and Liz's chance-meeting blossomed into dating by the end of that year. They were married in 1989 and the South Carolinian became part of the Alabama Gang.

She would bear Davey two children, Krista Marie, born in December 1989, and Robert Grey, born in July 1991.

Liz enjoyed only four years with Davey. During the time, she was forced to share him with the world.

Davey's moments out of racing's spotlight were few, but they were precious moments, his cousin Tommy said.

It was his attempt to squeeze more of those moments into his life - by the purchase of a helicopter that would save time between appointments -

Davey gets some friendly fishing advice from father Bobby and Red Farmer in 1989.

Davey and co-author Mike Bolton with 24 lb. stripe caught the day after the 1990 Winston 500.

that would eventually claim his life.

"Davey was gone 280 days out of the year," he said. "The past three years he made over 100 appearances a year for Texaco and Ford. A lot of those were two-hour autograph sessions that stretched into three- and four-hour sessions. Davey wouldn't leave anyone without an autograph.

"Davey had almost no time to himself, but when he got that time, he loved it. He built that new house (8,400 square feet) and settled in it in January. He built three lakes on it. He stocked those lakes with fish. He was going to enjoy that.

"He loved taking the kids swimming in the lake. It wasn't deep, and he'd put life jackets on the kids and get them out in the middle. He loved that.

"When Davey finally got home he didn't want to leave home. He didn't go out to eat or to the movies. He enjoyed spending time with his family."

Davey's big release was hunting and fishing, Tommy said.

"Hunting and fishing was his way of getting away from everything," Tommy said. "He was a great lover of the outdoors. He really didn't care if he shot a deer or caught a fish. He enjoyed getting away from the ringing telephone and the craziness of racing.

"Every year at the first of the year he would get the calendar before I could get to it and mark through December and January. Those were his months to hunt, and I wasn't allowed to schedule anything those two months except testing."

Davey said those two months belonged to him.

"We have a long season," he said last January. "The season doesn't really end anymore. We had the final race the third weekend in November. We tested at Daytona twice and Talladega once. When February begins, it's full speed ahead again.

"Getting away to the woods is my only escape. It's the only place the telephone doesn't ring," Davey said at that time. "Liz understands. She knows that's my thing."

Unlike many drivers who have hobbies they play at, Davey was a top-notch hunter and fisherman. He amazed the experts with his skills.

One of Davey's frequent hunting and fishing companions was Dennis Smith, host of the nationally syndicated outdoors show "Outdoors South."

"I have a lot of celebrities on my show, but none like Davey," Smith said early in 1993. "You have to show a lot of the celebrities everything to do, but Davey is as good a hunter and fisherman as I've ever seen.

"He's excellent with a bow, and that takes practice. I don't know when he has time to practice.

"But the most impressive thing to me about Davey is that even though he doesn't hunt and fish as much as he would like to, he's a true sportsman. He's not going to shoot something just to be

News staff photo by Mike Bolton

Davey talks hunting with former Auburn football star Terry Henley, while turkey hunting in South Alabama in 1991.

Davey and Dale Earnhardt had a few confrontations off the track, too. They are shown here before the obstacle course event in the 1991 Buckmasters Classic as Buckmasters founder Jackie Bushman looks on.

shooting. I've seen him pass up a lot of deer when he knows he might not get to go again for a while."

One hunting trip will forever stick in Smith's mind because it showed what kind of person Davey was, he said.

"I was with him one time when he wounded a deer," Smith said. "It was dark and one of those deals where he absolutely had to catch a plane. But he refused to leave before he found that deer. He walked through the woods throughout the night before he finally found it.

"A lot of celebrities would have said 'I've got to go. Ya'll find it.'"

Smith got to see Davey's true skills - and conservation-minded nature - while filming a show in 1990.

"Davey caught a 10-pound bass," Smith said. "We got it on film. Davey got that fish in, held it up to the camera and put it back into the water to swim away. Not many people would have done that."

One of Davey's favorite weeks every year came when he participated in the Buckmasters Classic, a hunting skills superstar-type competition held every year at the Southern Sportsman Hunting Lodge in Hayneville, Ala. The made-for-television event is featured on the Nashville Network as part of the Buckmasters television show.

Buckmasters founder Jackie Bushman put Davey on the roster six years ago. He was an instant hit with the participants and fans.

"Dale Earnhardt was in our first Buckmasters Classic, and the following year I went to the Charlotte race as a guest of Dale," said Bushman. "We were in Dale's condo overlooking the fourth turn and Richard Childress came in the room and said he had somebody with him who looked like a

Fishing was Davey's getaway and a sport that he approached with the same gusto as his racing.

teenager. I wasn't a racing fan and didn't know who it was. Richard introduced him as Davey Allison."

Bushman was conducting an interview with Earnhardt. Davey popped a tape of the previous year's Buckmasters Classic into the VCR.

"When it was over he asked what he had to do to get an invitation," Bushman said. "He said he'd do anything."

That was the beginning of a six-year run in which Davey competed in the Classic - a week that became one of his favorite of the year.

"Bo Jackson beat Davey in the obstacle course that first year, and that fired Davey up," Bushman remembers. "Davey didn't like to get beaten. He came back the next year and beat Bo."

The obstacle course involves participants putting on hunting clothes and boots and racing around a track on a four-wheeler. When Jackson got to the

first station that second year, he found his boot laces tied together. Davey was the culprit.

Davey went on to have classic confrontations in the obstacle course event with Earnhardt. Earnhardt beat Davey in 1990. Davey won the event in 1991.

"Davey liked being a team captain," Bushman said. "He took it serious. Two years ago he had to leave on Friday to test, but he flew back in late Friday night so he could participate on Saturday.

"Last year, he had to go test somewhere and his plane broke down. He chartered a plane to come back."

Bushman said many of the past contestants, including Davey's buddy New York Yankee Wade Boggs, called to express shock over his death.

"It's going to be tough without Davey," Bushman said. "There will be a big void there next year. We're going to rename the obstacle course event after him in his memory."

There was another side to Davey that wasn't well-publicized because he didn't want it to be. He donated thousands of dollars to charity. But more importantly, he donated his time.

Like their father, Davey and Clifford had been Boy Scouts. Even though their scouting days ended in 1976, the Allison family's loyalty to the Scouting program continues.

"The Allison family really got involved in scouting in 1977," said Jim Tinker, council executive for the Birmingham Council of Boy Scouts. "The Allisons have an annual fundraiser for the friends of scouting every year at Bobby Allison's house to raise money for Scouts in the western section of Birmingham.

"They had one in May and Bobby and Davey were there. In all, I guess the Allisons have been responsible for us raising $200,000 for Scouting.

"Davey was scheduled to speak at a Scout boost-ers breakfast at 7:30 on the morning he died. We tried to cancel the breakfast, but we had people coming in from out of state. We got word of Davey's death during the breakfast."

Davey had a special place in his heart for kids, said Tommy. If those kids were handicapped, Davey often went the extra mile. That was never so evident than earlier this year in Martinsville when 12-year-old Nikki Wilfong, of Danville, Va., finally got to meet her hero.

Allison took time from his qualifying schedule to host Nikki at the track. She had an adventure most kids only dream about.

Before qualifying, Davey picked her up and put her in the pace car for a spin around the track.

"That's all she talked about," said Nikki's grandmother, Dorothy Kashavsky. "And if that wasn't enough, she got two letters from Davey. She was beside herself.

"When she heard the news that Davey had been hurt in a helicopter crash and was injured, she sat

Photo courtesy of the Allison family

Davey and admiring fan, Tyler Sontag, chat at Daytona in 1991.

down and wrote him a letter in braille that night. She got up the next morning and turned on the TV and heard Davey had died. It broke her heart. She cried and cried."

Nikki by far was not the only child Davey touched.

Wheelchair-confined Tyler Sontag, who suffers from chronic respiratory failure and arthrogroyposis, a muscle disease, was at Daytona three years ago when Davey picked him out of a crowd and went over and talked with him.

Davey stayed in contact with the youngster. In July, he invited Tyler to Daytona as his guest.

"Davey was talking with Jeff Gordon explaining how you get through the turns at Daytona," Tyler's mother, Elizabeth recalled. "He stopped and leaned over to Tyler and said 'I'm telling him some of my secrets, but not all of them.' It was so cute."

Davey stayed in contact with the youngster the past year and sent him a box of goodies - Davey Allison hats and shirts, his mother said.

"It broke Tyler's heart when he heard Davey died," Mrs. Sontag said. "He cried Tuesday morning when he heard the news and again Thursday when he saw the tributes on television.

Jim and Vicki Simmons of Apopka, Fla., credits Davey with saving the life of her son, Jimbo.

The 21-year-old cerebral palsy victim, who has been deaf since he was six days old, was diagnosed with a deteriorating brain stem in November 1991, and was listed as terminal.

Mrs. Simmons wrote Allison telling him of her son's love of racing and that he was a big Davey Allison fan.

She was surprised four or five days later when Davey called. She was even more surprised in January 1992 when Davey called again and invited her son to be his guest at time trials for the Daytona 500. Jimbo spent a day with Allison in Daytona that year. In 1993, Davey invited Jimbo to the Daytona 500 again and this time he spent five days with Allison.

"Davey meant everything to my son," Mrs. Simmons said. "At the time Davey first called, my son was under constant care and would sometimes breathe only once every three minutes. He was totally paralyzed.

"After he heard from Davey, he made a dramatic change. He would get us to dress him up in the Davey Allison clothes Davey sent him before each time there was a race on television, His blood pressure would go up and his respiration would go up."

While Jimbo was visiting Davey in Daytona in early 1993, a miracle happened, she said.

"We got a call from a doctor in Baltimore who had seen Jimbo's records," she said. "She said the other doctors had misdiagnosed his problem. He had fallen in the shower and broken his neck and that was the problem.

"He's in rehabilitation now and walking again.

"Before Jimbo heard from Davey he was shut up in his room. Davey got him enthused. Davey made him feel like he was the only person in the world he cared about, and that kept Jimbo going until we got the correct diagnosis.

"I know when Davey died we lost a race car driver. But we also lost a person who really made a difference."

"I know when Davey died we lost a race car driver. But we also lost a person who really made a difference."

—Vicki Simmons, mother of child whose life was changed by Davey

"Sometimes, we tend to allow the tragedy and loss to overshadow his life. He had family. He had friends. He pursued the career he always wanted…He considered himself the luckiest guy in the world."

> —*Father Louis Giardino,*
> *pastor of St. Aloysius Catholic Church*

Chapter Nine

The Final Days

Monday, July 12, 1993

Davey Allison and Red Farmer and a half-dozen friends took their seats at their traditional table in the back of the Iceberg Restaurant in Hueytown. Memorabilia of the Allison family's greatest triumphs served as a backdrop on the wall behind the table. These were home folks.

Waitress Lisa Buchanan took Davey's order, but only out of courtesy. Davey always ordered the same thing - fried catfish and home-grown fries. This day was no different.

The lunchtime crowd was piling into the restaurant. Several customers dropped by the table to congratulate Davey on a job well done the day before in the Slick 50 300, the inaugural NASCAR Winston Cup race at New Hampshire International Speedway.

Allison was feeling good, despite the fact the past 48 hours had been incredibly hectic. His happi-ness could be attributed to events of the past weekend. It had given indications of being a frustrating one, but had turned out much better.

In Saturday's practice session in New Hampshire, Allison and his crew could not get the Texaco Havoline Ford Thunderbird up to speed. Sunday looked to be another of those days in what was proving to be a less than successful season - at least by Davey's standards.

Crew chief Larry McReynolds and the rest of the crew worked hard into the late hours Saturday, however. And on Sunday, Davey's car was dialed in when the race started. Davey worked his way to the front on lap 245 of the 300-lap event. It appeared he was heading to his second victory of the year.

Michael Waltrip's car lost a piece of a wheel hub on lap 271, and the debris on the track brought out the caution flag. Davey and Rusty Wallace pitted at the same time, but Wallace narrowly edged Davey

Dale Earnhardt displays a number 28 flag in the victory lane after winning the Miller 500 NASCAR race at Pocono International Raceway in memory of fellow racing driver Davey Allison.

out of the pits. When the green flag fell on lap 274, Wallace led the rest of the way for his first victory since his horrifying crash at the finish line in the Winston 500 earlier in the year. Mark Martin had sneaked past Davey at the end, pushing him back to third place.

"They had to throw the caution," Davey said afterward. "It was just an unlucky break for us. If that hadn't happened, they wouldn't have caught us."

Davey was never content with third place. But it was better than he could have hoped for on a Saturday when the car had barely been able to get around the track.

Following the race, Bobby Allison, Davey's team owner Robert Yates, McReynolds and long-time family friend Neil Bonnett hopped into Davey's airplane for the long flight home. Allison dropped McReynolds and Yates off in Charlotte, and the Alabama Gang arrived in Birmingham late in the night.

Allison had awakened early Monday at his new 8,400-square-foot home in Hueytown to take care of some of the never-ending, nitpicking details that complicated his life. He told his wife, Liz, good-bye. Then he promised his 3-year-old daughter Krista that when he returned home that afternoon he'd take her swimming in Grandaddy Bobby's pool.

Allison's first stop that morning was Bill's Farmhouse Restaurant in Hueytown, his usual breakfast stop when he was in town. He then headed to the Allison racing shops where his Busch Grand National car was being built. He was scheduled to test the car two days later at Talladega. The final mechanical touches were being done so the car could be put in the paint shop. Davey found an A-frame on the car he didn't like and instructed the crew to replace it with a shorter one. A crew member went out to the truck to get another, and Allison pitched in and helped replace it.

Davey took a mid-morning break to make the 400-yard trip up the hill behind the shop to visit the construction site of the helipad he was having built. Allison had purchased a Hughes 369 HS helicopter from Stevens Racing in Mooresville, N.C., just three weeks before. Allison told everyone he had wanted the copter to cut travel time - to give himself a few

more precious minutes to spend with his family. The copter could also be used to get him to his uncle Donnie's farm in Faunsdale quickly during hunting season, saving him just a few more of those precious minutes in his numerous trips to the Birmingham airport - where his nine-passenger, twin turboprop Piper Cheyenne was stored.

Few bought the explanation. Davey wanted something new to play with, they believed.

"A lot of people begged him not to buy the helicopter," long-time Allison family friend Horace Gray remembers now. "That just fueled the fire."

Davey liked what he saw of the helipad. He gave construction foreman Barry Shipman the go-ahead to pour the concrete.

Davey returned to the Allison shop, which is just a stone's throw from Bobby Allison's home where Davey was raised. The home of Mom and Pop Allison, Davey's grandparents, is just across the street. Red Farmer's home is just a few doors up the street.

Davey was antsy to get the work completed on his Busch Grand National car. He and Farmer had already decided to take the helicopter to Talladega that afternoon to watch David Bonnett, Neil Bonnett's son, test his Busch Grand National car. After several hours of work on the car, it was ready to be rolled over to the paint shop.

Davey's cousin Tommy, the son of Bobby's brother, said, "Let's get some lunch."

The Iceberg was busy as usual and Davey's entrance caused the usual commotion. Davey, as usual, teased the waitresses. Several times he jokingly prodded them to hurry.

"We've got to jump in the helicopter and get out of here," he said.

The gang left the Iceberg at approximately 12:45 - 45 minutes after they entered - and returned to the shop where Davey took care of several more details. Gray was leaving the shop and Davey went outside with him.

"Me and Red are going to Talladega in the helicopter. Come on and go with us," he told Gray. Gray explained that his wife's car was in the shop and he had to take care of it. Allison promised to be back "A little after four," but Gray said he had to pick up the car before then.

"I'll be back here Wednesday, and I'm taking you up in the helicopter," Allison told him.

"I'll do it then," Gray promised.

It was the last time Gray would ever see Davey Allison alive.

Davey and Farmer drove to the Birmingham Airport. After fueling the helicopter, they were in the air at 3:15 p.m. They were greeted by bluebird skies as they flew north. Interstate 20 served as their guide. Just 30 minutes later, they were circling Talladega Superspeedway looking for a place to land.

Weeks of little rainfall had left most of the speedway infield parched and dusty. Davey chose to put the copter down in the asphalt media parking lot, which was surrounded by a 12-foot-high chain-link fence topped with barbed wire.

Almost a dozen people - mostly track workers - gathered to watch the copter land. What they witnessed will forever be etched in their minds.

The landing appeared normal as Davey brought the copter down. He decided to turn the helicopter so it would be heading out in the right direction. But six inches above the asphalt the copter began swaying side-to-side in a pendulum motion. Suddenly the copter rose to 25 feet above the ground and began spinning counterclockwise. It then banked hard left, turned upside down and plummeted hard onto an asphalt road adjacent to the media parking lot. The copter tumbled and eventually came to a rest on Farmer's side. It happened in a matter of seconds.

The tail rotor apparently caught the fence surrounding the media lot as the copter fell to the ground, evidenced by a section of the rotor that remained entwined in the barbed wire of the damaged fence. Pieces or wreckage were thrown 75 feet away.

Farmer was stunned and injured, but he'd been upside down before and kept his thoughts. "Davey, let's get out of here, the motor's still running," Farmer screamed as he tried to free himself from the shoulder harnesses.

Davey did not answer.

"Davey was hanging upside down, but I couldn't undo the seat belts because he'd fall on me," Farmer recalled hours after the crash. "I knocked the glass out and crawled out.

"We had just gassed up before we left, and I was afraid it would catch fire," Farmer recalled later.

Neil Bonnett was the first to the scene and Farmer screamed for him to get Davey out before it caught on fire.

"I go out there and see this mass of metal," Bonnett told ESPN later. "The motor is going full speed . . . The engine is running full power. I run around there and see somebody trying to get out of the bottom of the aircraft. I couldn't see who it was, then I recognized Red Farmer.

"I go and try to get Red out. It was a mass of confusion. I probably did everything wrong. People were saying to get away, it might blow up. I said I had to get back in there and get Davey. It's the most helpless I ever felt. I couldn't get him out."

The helicopter did not burn, but the motor-minus the rotor blades which were broken off in the crash - continued to run for 25 minutes after the crash. Bonnett said, "It was the loudest noise I ever heard." An aviation mechanic from the airport adjacent to the track was finally called to shut the engine off.

Meanwhile, a track nurse entered the aircraft and administered to Davey as he was being cut from the wreckage by emergency workers.

Davey and Farmer were taken to the J.L. Hardwick Infield Care Center, which is manned with medical personnel during all races and test sessions. They immediately determined that Davey's head injuries were life-threatening and Farmer's multiple injuries were serious. Carraway Methodist Medical Center in Birmingham was called, and the hospital dispatched two Lifesaver helicopters. Rescue workers in the infield hospital started an IV in Davey and began tending to Farmer's injuries as they waited the 20 minutes for the helicopters to arrive. They said Allison was never conscious.

Farmer suffered a broken collarbone, a broken nose and broken ribs and was listed as critical upon arriving in Birmingham. Doctors found that Davey had a broken pelvis, lung damage and an "acute, subdural hemotoma," a blood clot on the brain. He was rushed into surgery where holes were drilled in his skull to relieve pressure on the brain and the blood clot was removed.

Davey was then taken to the neurological inten-

Fans line the route of the funeral procession holding signs, checkered flags, and wearing Davey Allison fan T-shirts.

sive care unit where his family, including Bobby and Judy and his wife Liz gathered at his side in a scene all too familiar to the Allison family. The family was given little sign for hope. But they stood by his bedside and talked to him throughout the night, even though he was in a coma.

Those closest to Davey, including car-owner Robert Yates, raced to his side during the night. When Bobby Allison hugged Yates in the intensive care waiting room and told him "He's hurt worse than I was," Yates braced for the worse.

"I wanted to ask the doctors if there was a situation where people recovered from this," Yates said following the news from Bobby. "I didn't ask that. I didn't feel like I would get a positive answer. I was afraid to ask."

The Allisons prayed for a miracle throughout the night, as did thousands of fans across the nation. At 4 the following morning, Davey took a turn for the worse.

He was pronounced dead at 7 a.m. The Allison family's final act of giving was to donate Davey's organs "so others could live."

The announcement of Davey's death plunged Alabama into a period of mourning unlike any experienced since the death of Bear Bryant more than 10 years before. Within minutes of the announcement, signs expressing grief and love for the Allison family were erected in front yards and in front of businesses across Alabama. Birmingham radio station WZZK played Garth Brooks' "The Dance," and dedicated the song to Davey. Hundreds of listeners drove to work with tears streaming down their faces. It was the same scene in offices across the state where Davey Allison fans gathered around radios and televisions.

Flags from Hueytown City Hall to the Alabama capitol in Montgomery were lowered to half-staff.

Thousands of Alabama motorists turned on their headlights in memory of Davey.

As news of Davey's death began to filter out across the country, phones rang at newspapers and television stations nationwide with callers begging to be told that what they had heard was an error. The switchboard at The Birmingham News was flooded with calls from as far away as California.

ESPN sent many shaken Davey Allison fans to bed that night with a tearful, 30-minute tribute. By mid-afternoon the following day, the Hueytown Post Office had received 1,800 pieces of mail addressed to P.O. Box 28.

Meanwhile, few failed to notice the irony in Davey losing his life at Talladega Superspeedway, the site of many of the greatest moments in his career. It was at Talladega that Davey won his first superspeedway pole in the April 30, 1983 ARCA race. That win gave him his first superspeedway victory. It was Talladega where he started his first Winston Cup race in the 1985 Talladega 500 and it was Talladega where Davey won his first Winston Cup race, the 1987 Winston 500.

In all, Davey won one ARCA 200, three ARCA 500K races, three Winston 500's and one IROC race at Talladega. Allison is Talladega's all-time winner.

Early Tuesday, the morning following the accident, investigators from the National Traffic Safety Board and the Federal Aviation Administration began the tedious task of sorting through the wreckage in search of an answer for what caused the crash. The four rotor blades had been torn away and most of the tail section had been ripped off, but the main cabin had pretty much remained intact. The helicopter, first built for military use in 1961, is known for its ability to survive crashes. There is one documented case of this type of helicopter crashing head-on into a mountain at 135 mph during the Vietnam War. The pilot survived.

The four-seat, 1,100-pound aircraft has a protective cage that surrounds the front passengers. Yet Davey died, while his passenger, Red Farmer, was able to walk away under his own power. For many, it was hard to understand.

NTSB investigator Roff

Birmingham News Photo

Sasser told reporters on the afternoon following the crash that preliminary investigation had revealed no mechanical defects in the helicopter. However, he stressed that the investigation was still in the preliminary stages. He said a report on the suspected cause of the crash would not be released until some time in 1994.

During the same hour as NTSB officials called a press conference to discuss the crash, funeral plans for Davey were being announced in Birmingham.

The Wednesday-night wake was set for St. Aloysius Catholic Church in Bessemer, the church the Allison family attended and the same church where the body of Clifford Allison had lay just 11 months before. A Who's Who of the racing world were among the crowd of 4,000 that attended the wake. But the bulk of the crowd was made up of those who never met Davey. Many wore their Davey Allison T-shirts.

The crowd for the 6:30 p.m. wake began gathering at 2:30. Bessemer police reported cars parked along the roadway up to two miles away. Red Farmer, Darrell Waltrip, Bill Elliott, Jeff Gordon, Ken Schrader, Brett Bodine, Bobby and Terry Labonte, Hut Stricklin, Mario Andretti, Junior Johnson and Alabama Governor Jim Folsom were among those who attended the wake.

Father Louis Giardino, who pastors St. Aloysius Church and led the rosary at Clifford Allison's service, told the crowd: "Your presence here, your dedication and devotion to Davey and his family, your willingness to be part of this, is very moving and very supportive."

The next morning, the closed-casket service opened with "Amazing Grace" and closed with "How Great Thou Art." A red-framed portrait of Davey in his racing suit sat atop the casket. Liz Allison took the portrait with her when she left the church.

Hundreds attended the funeral the following day. More than 600 packed themselves into the church and another 500 had to listen to the service via loudspeakers outside in the sweltering sun.

Giardino told the crowd: "Davey Allison is the luckiest person in the world. Sometimes, we tend to allow the tragedy and loss to overshadow his life. He had family. He had friends. He pursued the career he always wanted. He had it all. He considered himself the luckiest guy in the world."

NASCAR Chaplain Max Helton told the crowd: "He beat us all to heaven. What a race to win."

Hundreds of Davey Allison supporters lined the roads from St. Aloysius Church to Highland Memorial Gardens in Bessemer, which would be Davey's final resting place. Clifford and "Pop" Allison are also buried there.

Several mourners held signs while others waved checkered flags as Davey's funeral procession passed.

In the shade of a towering oak just 10 feet from the woods Davey loved so much, he was laid to rest. Country singer Joe Diffie, a close friend of Davey's, sang his favorite song - "Ships That Don't Come In" - bringing many in attendance to tears.

Liz Allison closed the service by hugging Davey's casket, then placed a dozen red roses on top before departing. Hundreds of mourners stayed to walk by and touch Davey's casket before they left.

An era was over.

The Pocono 500 that followed three days later marked the first time since 1975 - more than 18 years - that a NASCAR Winston Cup race did not have an Allison in the field.

"I can remember praying for things I didn't get, but I can remember praying for things I did get. I remember becoming oriented pretty early that God doesn't always do things the way we want them done."

—*Bobby Allison*

Epilogue

It was 1976, and he had been in a racing crash.

There was no feeling in his feet. He thought he might no longer have any feet.

"Has racing been worth this, losing my feet?" he asked himself.

He pondered the question, thought about the good times, and the bad times.

"Yes," he answered his own question. "It has been worth it."

The Winston Cup star was driving in a sports-man event on a third-mile track at Elko, Minn., on July 10. There was nothing unusual about that. He enjoyed racing, enjoyed visiting short tracks all over the nation - and enjoyed earning the show money that promoters paid him to challenge the local hot-shots.

"Of course I get compensated," he once said, explaining that his return to the short tracks did involve love of the sport, not just money, "but other drivers could do the same thing, and don't."

The motor in a car ahead of him blew, laying down a sheet of oil. Bobby Allison's tires got in it, and his car hit the wall - at the worst place possible. It contacted an abutment in a gate opening. Esti-

Birmingham News Photo

Bobby and Judy Allison

Associated Press Photo

Davey talks with his father, Bobby, at Pocono Raceway a year after his father's accident there.

his face.

He remained in a Minnesota hospital for four days before being released. Surely he would be out of action for a long time.

But as someone once said, "Football players play hurt; race drivers play broken."

On July 15, Bobby's friend Neil Bonnett qualified Bobby's Mercury on the pole for the Winston Cup race at Nashville. On July 17, Bobby started the race so that he could, as NASCAR rules required, earn the points for the car's finish.

His crewmen began helping him into the racer 15 minutes before the start of the event, plenty of time to exercise the utmost caution. They didn't want one of the broken ribs to puncture a lung.

mates were that the concrete gave about18 inches, and in that 18 inches Bobby's car went from 85 miles per hour to a dead stop.

As Big Bill France used to say about his ultra-fast 2.66-mile Talladega Superspeedway when it was new: "In racing, it isn't how fast you go - it's how fast you stop."

Rescue workers found Bobby bleeding and unconscious. They worked desperately to free him from the wreckage.

He awoke on the way to the hospital. He was in terrible pain. His uniform was soaked in blood. He touched his face and found a deep cut and began to realize that he was seriously injured.

He had suffered three broken bones in his left foot, two broken bones in his right foot, three broken ribs, a broken nose, two facial fractures and a fracture of the eye socket with resulting double vision. It took forty stitches to close the wound in

Bobby fulfilled the requirement to get his points and immediately pitted so Bonnett could drive the car. Special cloth handles had been sewn onto Bobby's uniform to facilitate removing him from the car. Bonnett finished in seventh place.

Bonnett relieved him at Pocono, too. But on Aug. 8, less than a month after the accident, Bobby required no relief driver at Talladega.

The Allison family has experienced many victories and a national championship. But it also has been battered with so much injury and death that driver Darrell Waltrip was moved to say, "When I think of Judy Allison, I think about Job in the Bible and all he endured."

Donnie Allison, Bobby's brother, wrecked in the

1981 World 600 at Charlotte. Though he drove occasionally after that, the accident virtually ended his career.

In 1988, Bobby's car was T-boned at Pocono. His recovery has been long and slow, and there are still gaps in his memory. He owns his own race team, but he hasn't driven since, except in an exhibition. He still has not declared himself retired as a driver, though.

Clifford Allison, Davey's 27-year-old brother, was killed in a racing practice crash at Michigan Aug. 13, 1992. The same year, Davey's grandfather, Ed Allison - patriarch of the Peachfuzz Gang - died, and Davey was injured several times in wrecks, including a spectacular accident at Pocono.

On July 12, Davey's helicopter crashed at Talladega Superspeedway, site of some of his greatest accomplishments. He died the next day.

The Allisons hurt. Their friends hurt for them. Fans who never met them hurt.

Less than three weeks after Clifford's death, his mother Judy greeted an old newspaper friend at her home. She was cleaning out her cabinets and closets, stuffing 20 boxes with items for victims of Hurricane Andrew.

Excuse the mess, she said, as housewives have for centuries. "This has been good therapy for me."

The petite 50-year-old blonde took a seat in a recliner, finally able to talk about the loss of a son.

She touched her stomach and said, "Once you have that feeling of a baby, it's like he's still in there. It's been years, but you still feel four little flutters in there - and then it's like one day someone reaches in there and takes away one of those little flutters."

How does Judy Allison come to terms with the sport her men chose?

"It's hard to put into words," she said. "It's like an acceptance. When somebody is really determined you can tell it. When you realize they're going to do it whether you like it or not, you'd better join them or you're going to be out in left field. Some women can't make that acceptance, and they do get left behind."

During that same time, Bobby Allison talked to the newspaper friend about how his religion was helping him get through.

"The Catholic religion has been a plus to me

Birmingham News Photo

Davey drove with a heavily bandaged right arm in the 1992 Talladega 500.

through my career, because it helps you through the good times and the bad times.

"I can remember praying for things I didn't get, but I can remember praying for things I did get. I remember becoming oriented pretty early that God doesn't always do things the way we want them done."

His parents instilled religion in his life. "When I was in high school I would work with my father, and I'd see him pinch his fingers, or something would fall over and cause another four hours of work," Bobby said. "But I never heard him say a cuss word."

Though he still wasn't 100 percent after his crash of four years before - and though his father Ed and his son Clifford had died less than five months apart - Bobby didn't moan about the afflictions of his family.

"I can't do that," he said. "Christ died on that cross for us. They drove nails through His hands and feet. I learned since day one that heaven is the ultimate joy. I have to think in those terms."

Bobby's sons followed in his footsteps in a dangerous profession.

"The only thing I can say about that is how would I feel if either one was working in a factory or on a construction job, something he didn't want to do, and got killed?"

"…how would I feel if (either of my sons) was working in a factory or on a construction job, something he didn't want to do, and got killed?"

—Bobby Allison, reflecting on the dangerous profession of his family

"I wasn't ready for it to end, and I know he wasn't. But I consider myself lucky—and I know he did."

—*Tommy Allison*

CHRONOLOGY

1961
Born on February 25 in Hollywood, Fla. on the eve of Bobby's first Daytona 500 race.

1962
Davey's sister, Bonnie, was born Dec. 4.

1963
Moved with family to an apartment in Birmingham's West End.

1964
Davey's brother Clifford was born Oct. 20.

1967
Davey's sister Carrie was born May 3.

1968
Started first grade at St. Aloysius Catholic School.

1971
Notation on 4th grade report card from St. Aloysius read: "'He thinks too much about racing."

1972
Notation on 5th grade report card from St. Aloysius read: "He daydreams about racing in the classroom."

1973
Began, at age 12, as a 6th grader sweeping floors, sorting nuts and bolts, at Bobby Allison Racing for 50 cents an hour. At the time, Bobby Allison Racing was producing up to 100 race cars annually.

1975
Graduated from St. Aloysius Catholic School.

1976
Responding to preoccupation with racing, parents demanded Davey earn a high school diploma, "not a GED," before embarking on racing career . . . Played organized baseball and basketball . . . Preferred football, played tailback and defensive cornerback at Hueytown Community Center.

1977

Father, campaigning AMC Matador in Winston Cup as an independent, couldn't afford to pay for extra help . . . Davey went to school, bagged groceries at the Food Giant in Hueytown from 3:30 to 9 p.m., ate dinner quickly and went to work for free at Bobby Allison Racing . . . Often quit just in time to shower and head for class.

1978

Attended summer classes between junior and senior years of high school to ensure early completion.

1979

Completed high school studies in January, started full time at Bobby Allison Racing . . . Allowed use of shop and equipment to build first race car, but only after 5 p.m. . . . Constructed 1967 Chevrolet Nova from ground up.

Started first race (April 22) at 5/8-mile paved oval in Birmingham. . . . Drove 1972 Chevrolet II Nova borrowed from Donnie and rebuilt with help from cousin Kenny . . . Finished fifth in 20-lap Limited Sportsman feature.

Won first race in sixth start, at Birmingham (May 5), with Dad in pits . . . Bobby won Winston Cup race at Talladega, Ala., the next day . . . Missed race to attend high school commencement.

First race against father, at Jackson, Miss. (Sept. 1) . . . Davey finished sixth . . . Bobby started fourth, but finished 16th after mechanical trouble. Also competed at Dothan, Huntsville, Montgomery and Sayre, Ala., plus Pensacola, Fla. . . . Started 34 races, finished season with five wins, 20 top-five, 29 top-10 and $3,400 in winnings.

1980

Continued in Limited Sportsman on short tracks of deep South . . . Started first superspeedway race . . . Drove Bobby's Matador in 150-mile ARCA event at Brooklyn, Mich. (Sept. 20) . . . Started first NASCAR Winston West race at Phoenix (Nov. 26).

1981

Moved up to NASCAR Grand American (Now All-American) at Birmingham and Montgomery . . . Started 37th (last) in ARCA race at Daytona Beach, Fla., and finished sixth . . . Traveled extensively to compete on All Pro circuit, aided by volunteer group of friends and relatives dubbed the "Peachfuzz Gang," ages 15-19.

1983

Earned first superspeedway pole and first superspeedway victory in ARCA race at Talladega (April 30) . . . Started first Busch Grand National race at Rockingham, N.C., (March 5) and finished 25th . . . In four more starts at Darlington, S.C., and Charlotte, N.C., earned one top-five and three top-10s . . . Entered only a handful of NASCAR Dash races, but tied series champion Michael Waltrip for Most Popular Driver . . . Also competed in All Pro, ASA and Grand American.

1984

Earned ARCA Rookie of the Year . . . Won ARCA superspeedway races at Atlanta and Talladega, plus short track race at Macon, Ga. . . . Missed one race while on honeymoon and lost series title by 25 points to Bob Dotter . . . Won first ARCA Bill France Triple Crown award . . . Won NASCAR Grand American race at Birmingham . . . Scored three top-five finishes in six Busch Grand National starts . . . Also raced in All Pro, ASA, DIRT, Grand American and International Sedan (now Dash) series.

1985

Drastically reduced short track events to concentrate on longer distance superspeedway races . . . Won "about 45" short track feature races between 1979 and 1984.

Started first Winston Cup race at Talladega 500 (July 28) . . . Qualified 22nd and finished 10th in Hoss Ellington's Lancaster Tobacco Chevrolet, won $6,025 . . . Also entered Charlotte and Atlanta races in fall.

Won ARCA superspeedway races at Talladega (May 4) and Atlanta (June 2), plus short track show at Indianapolis . . . Finished third in final standings . . . At end of 1985, was ARCA's all-time leader on super speedways with four poles and six wins . . . Earned three poles, four wins at Talladega, one pole, two wins at Atlanta plus one pole, two wins on short tracks . . . Also competed in All Pro, Busch Grand National and Grand American.

1986

Started four Winston Cup races in spring for Sadler Bros. team at Richmond, Rockingham, Bristol, Tenn., and Darlington . . . Finished second in ARCA race at Talladega (May 3) . . . Junior Johnson picked him to sub for an injured Neil Bonnett at Talladega (July 27) . . . Started seventh, led twice and finished seventh.

1987

Hired by Ranier-Lundy Winston Cup team . . . Qualified second at 209-plus mph to become first rookie to start on front row for Daytona 500 . . . At second race of season, earned first Winston Cup pole at Rockingham in only 10th career Winston Cup race . . . Set new standard for Winston Cup rookies with five poles . . . Added three outside poles for eight front-row starts in all.

Won first Winston Cup race at Talladega (May 3) in only 14th career start . . . Became one of only five since 1958 to triumph in first season . . . Two races later at Dover, Del., became only driver in Winston Cup history to win twice in rookie season . . . Narrowly missed three more wins, finishing second by .15-, one- and two-second margins . . . Earned Rookie of the Year, set and still holds record for rookie winnings ($361,060) and finished 21st in final standings all with only 22 starts in 29 races . . . Founded Davey Allison Racing Enterprises Busch Grand National team in December.

1988

Finished second to father, Bobby, at Daytona 500 . . . Won back-to-back pole positions at Talladega and Charlotte in May . . . Bobby critically injured in first-lap accident at Pocono, Pa., (June 19) . . . Despite helping direct father's recovery and new family responsibilities, won third Winston Cup race at Michigan (Aug. 21).

Met Elizabeth Mayson in the back of pickup truck at a charity autograph session in Charleston, S.C., before the Southern 500 . . . Won fourth race from pole at Richmond (Sept. 11) after Bobby gave starting command over public address, via telephone from rehabilitation center in Alabama . . . Finished eighth in Winston Cup points, won $844,532.

Team became Robert Yates Racing on Oct. 1, when crew chief/engine builder Yates purchased operation from Harry Ranier.

1989

Earned fifth Winston Cup victory by winning Talladega (May 7) for second time . . . Posted sixth win at Daytona (July 1) and won pole at Dover in September . . . Married "Liz" . . . Finished 11th in Winston Cup points, won $640,956. . . First child, Krista Marie, born on Dec. 24.

1990

Scored seventh and eighth Winston Cup wins, at Bristol (April 8) by 8/10ths of an inch over Mark Martin and at Charlotte (Oct. 7) . . . Finished 13th in Winston Cup points, won $640,684.

1991

Breakthrough campaign . . . Opened season with back-to-back poles at Daytona and Richmond, but 21st in points when Larry McReynolds became crew chief after four races. McReynolds led team to five victories, at Charlotte (May 26), Sonoma, Calif., (June 9), Michigan (June 23), Rockingham (Oct. 23), Phoenix (Nov. 3) and pole at Darlington (Sept. 1) . . . Also won The Winston (May 19) all-star race from pole.

Davey led more races (23), more times (73) for more miles (1,879.12) than any other Winston Cup driver . . . Collected numerous post-season awards . . . Finished third in final standings by four points to Ricky Rudd, won career high $1,732,924 . . . Led Busch Grand National race at Dover (June 1) with one lap to go, but fuel pickup failed . . . Second child, Robert Grey, was born on July 30.

1992

Astounding dichotomy of highs and lows . . . Despite wrecking primary car in practice, rebounded to win season-opening Daytona 500 by STP . . . Joined father, Bobby, a three-time winner, to become second father-son duo (Lee-Richard Petty) to win the 500.

Grandfather Ed "Pop" Allison, Bobby's father and patriarch of the "Peachfuzz Gang" with which Davey started racing, died April 1.

Led 50 laps at Bristol, before an oil-line fitting broke and sent his car skating hard into the wall (April 5) . . . Went home to bury "Pop" with separated cartilage, fractured ribs, a bruised lung plus torn ligaments and muscles in his right shoulder . . . Because of Davey's injuries, Jimmy Hensley qualified (seventh) and practiced car at North Wilksboro, N.C.

Taking advantage of superior pit work by his teammates, Davey grabbed lead with 87 laps to go and, despite severe leg cramps, held off Rusty Wallace for the victory (April 12) . . . Dedicated win to "Pop."

A cut right front tire sent car into wall at Martinsville, Va., (April 26), re-injuring ribs . . . Qualified second, led 110 of 188 laps to win Winston 500 at Talladega (May 3) . . . Now, a win at either Charlotte in May or Darlington in September would earn the Winston Million . . . Started from pole, led 160 of 200 laps and won Brooklyn (June 21).

Joined select group of NASCAR Winston Cup drivers to participate in testing at Indianapolis Motor Speedway.

Despite spending two nights in Charlotte hospital for treatment of a virus, sped to pole and led 115 laps at Pocono (July 19) before contact with Darrell Waltrip on lap 149 sent car into a spectacular, 11-flip accident . . . That night, surgeons installed two plates in his broken forearm and pins in his dislocated, shattered wrist . . . Also sustained a broken collarbone and severe swelling and bruising of his face and head . . . For first time in 1992, trailed for Winston Cup title by 19 points to Bill Elliott.

Six days later, practiced at 188+ mph in preparation for race at Talladega (July 26) . . . Relief driver Bobby Hillin qualified car third . . . Davey started, then yielded to Hillin during a brief rain shower caution on fifth lap . . . Hillin led for 30 laps and finished third to put Davey back in lead for title . . . Two weeks later, Dorsey Shroeder drove in relief at Watkins Glen, N.Y.

Younger brother Clifford, was killed in a crash during a Busch Series practice at Brooklyn (Aug. 13) . . . The next day, Davey qualified third, then gutted out first complete race since Pocono crash for fifth-place finish (Aug. 16).

After leading 72 laps, was in excellent position to win final leg of Winston Million at Darlington, S.C., (Sept. 6) when rain, just after Davey pitted for fuel, cut the race short and relegated him to a fifth-place finish.

Struggled to find combination in next five races and averaged 13th-place finish before scoring resurgent win at Phoenix (Nov. 1) to regain Winston Cup points lead by 30 over Alan Kulwicki.

Running sixth with less than 100 laps to go and in position to secure the title, Davey was caught in an accident triggered by Ernie Irvan . . . The wreck deprived him of the Winston Cup title and dropped him to third in points, his lowest ranking of the season.

Five victories tied him for series lead with Bill Elliott . . . Led the series in top-five finishes (17) . . .

Also led series in victories (tied at five), top-five finishes (17), laps led (1,362), miles led (2,315) and times led (tied at 50) . . . Also led in regular season winnings ($1,621,730) and set career earnings mark for single season ($1,955,628).

1993

Disappointing season with just one victory (Richmond) in 19 starts . . . Posted six top 5 finishes and eight top 10 finishes, winning $513,585 . . . Helicopter he was piloting crashed in infield of Talladega Superspeedway on July 12 . . . Died the morning of July 13.

The Record

Davey Allison's Winston Cup Record

Year	Races	Wins	Top 5	Top 10	Total won
1985	3	0	0	1	$10,615
1986	5	0	0	1	$24,190
1987	22	2	9	10	$361,060
1988	29	2	12	16	$844,532
1989	29	2	7	13	$640,956
1990	29	2	5	10	$640,684
1991	29	5	12	16	$1,732,924
1992	29	5	15	17	$1,955,628
1993	16	1	6	8	$513,585
Career:	164	19	66	93	$6,724,174

Davey Allison's Talladega Success
Eight wins is most by any driver

1983 - ARCA 500K	**1987** - Winston 500
1983 - ARCA 200	**1989** - Winston 500
1984 - ARCA 500K	**1992** - IROC
1985 - ARCA 500K	**1992** - Winston 500

The Allison Racing Family

Bobby Allison
Famed race car driver for more than four decades. Tied for third all-time with 84 Winston Cup victories in 717 races from 1961-1988. Won 1983 Winston Cup Championship, and was runner-up five other times. Won 1964 and 65 NASCAR modified titles. Formed own Winston Cup team, with three partners, in 1989. Lives in Hueytown, Ala., moving from south Florida more than 30 years ago. Father of late race car drivers Davey Allison and Clifford Allison.

Davey Allison
NASCAR race car driver. Began racing in 1979, with first victory at Birmingham International Raceway. Won first Winston Cup event in 1987. Talladega track's all-time leading winner with eight wins in ARCA, IROC and Winston Cup. Won 19 Winston Cup races, and finished third in Winston Cup points race in 1991 and 1992. Died in helicopter crash July 13, 1993 at age 32.

Clifford Allison
Son of Bobby Allison. Younger brother of Davey Allison. First raced in Birmingham in 1983. Was ARCA crew chief for Davey in 1984 and 85. Also served in father's crew from time to time. Late model track champion at Montgomery, Ala., in 1987. Recorded four top-five finishes and six top 10s in seven ARCA starts in 1992. Killed in Busch practice crash at Michigan International Speedway on August 13, 1992.

Donnie Allison
Bobby Allison's brother. Race car driver who earned 17 pole positions, 10 Winston Cup wins and $1,014,028 in 241 races from 1966 to 1988. Was 1967 Winston Cup Rookie of the Year, and 1970 Indianapolis 500 Rookie of the Year.

Tommy Allison, Jr.
Son of Bobby Allison's brother, Tommy Sr. Vice president of A-Star Promotions. General Manager of Davey Allison Racing Enterprises and Davey Allison Equipment. Also in charge of Davey's personal business.

Steve Allison
Tommy Allison Jr.'s younger brother. Aspiring driver; started in carts at 9. Advanced through classes to Late Models. Moved to Concord, N.C., in 1993 to pursue career.

Joe Allison
Tommy Allison Jr.'s youngest brother. Sometime crew member for Davey Allison's Busch team. Nation's top placekicker as a junior at Memphis State University in 1992. All American.

Kenny, Donald and Ronald Allison

Sons of Donnie Allison. Own Allison Brothers Racing that built Davey Allison's Grand National cars.

Hut Stricklin

Husband of Davey Allison's cousin, Pam. Pam is daughter of Donnie Allison. Stricklin is a race car driver for the Junior Johnson team. He drives the #27 McDonald's Ford.

Katherine "Kitty" and Edmond "Pop" Allison

Bobby and Donnie Allison's parents. One of the racing circuit's most beloved couples. Pop died April 1, 1992. Kitty, 86, attends races whenever possible.

About the Authors

Clyde Bolton, sports columnist of *The Birmingham News*, began covering auto racing for the paper in 1962. In 1985 he won the most prestigious prize in motorsports journalism, The Russ Catlin Award, for the best story of the year in the nation on Winston Cup Racing.

He is a 30-year friend of the Allison family, and he considers the 1988 Daytona 500 - in which Bobby Allison finished first and Davey Allison second - the most memorable sports event he has covered in 39 years in the newspaper business.

Clyde Bolton is the author of seven other non-fiction books - *Bolton's Best Stories of Auto Racing, the Crimson Tide, War Eagle, Unforgettable Days in Southern Football, They Wore Crimson, Silver Britches* and *The Basketball Tide* - and four novels - *Water Oaks, Ivy, And Now I See* and *The Lost Sunshine.*

He is currently writing a book on 25 years of racing at Talladega Superspeedway.

Clyde is married to the former Sandra Jean Griffin and they have three grown sons.

Mike Bolton, staff writer for *The Birmingham News*, began covering auto racing in the mid-1970's. He has won several awards, as well as a college scholarship, for his auto racing writings.

He has known the Allisons since he was five years old and was a frequent hunting and fishing companion of Davey's, and was Davey's hunting partner in the 1992 Buckmasters Classic.

One of his most memorable moments was taking Davey fishing and Davey catching his biggest fish ever - a 24-pound striped bass.

Mike is married to the former Beth Shryock and they have two children, Cory Michael and Lauren Elizabeth.